Developing Your People

Easy-to-use activities for improving management skills

Developing Your People

Easy-to-use activities for improving management skills

Mike Woodcock and Dave Francis

Gower

Published by
Gower Publishing Limited
Gower House
Croft Road
Aldershot
Hampshire GU11 3HR
England

Gower
Old Post Road
Brookfield
Vermont 05036
USA

Mike Woodcock and Dave Francis have asserted their right under the Copyright, Designs and Patents Act 1988 to be identified as the authors of this work.

British Library Cataloging in Publication Data
Woodcock, Mike
  Developing your people
  1. Industrial management 2. Executive ability
  I. Title II. Francis, Dave
  658

ISBN 0 566 07933 X

Library of Congress Cataloging-in-Publication Data
Woodcock, Mike.
    Developing your people: easy-to-use activities for improving
  management skills / Mike Woodcock and Dave Francis.
      p. cm.
    Includes index.
    ISBN 0–566–07933–X (hc)
    1. Management games. I. Francis, Dave. II. Title.
  HD30.26.W66 1997   96–52235
  658.4'0712404—DC21   CIP

Typeset in New Baskerville by Bournemouth Colour Press, Parkstone and printed in Great Britain by Hartnoll Ltd, Bodmin.

Contents

v

Preface

This book is being published in two versions: one for managers and the other for trainers.

The managers' version, *Developing Your People: Easy-to-use activities for improving management skills*, is especially timely. More managers are seeing the management of learning as a key task. Today, many managers take on the role of coaches and facilitators and the material in this book will provide a range of useful structured approaches. The authors believe that it is important to encourage managers to develop training skills; for too long it has been considered that learning and work are separate. It is time to develop a seamless integration between these two key activities.

The trainers' version, *Interventions for Developing Managerial Competencies*, contains additional guidance that professional trainers will find helpful. There is material on the role of the facilitator and the use of the instruments, activities and exercises within a 'classroom' environment.

Mike Woodcock
Dave Francis

Introduction

A new definition of 'management' is beginning to emerge. The 'craft' of management continues to develop as innovative managers, research institutes and business schools clarify what management will be like in future years. Our role as authors is to take leading-edge thinking, to simplify it and help individual managers develop their skills to deal with the massive changes which they confront. In this book we offer a bridge which links ordinary managers with evolving concepts of management. We do this by presenting a range of practical activities which managers can undertake to enhance skills, improve understanding and help reduce personal blockages.

Managers must become engaged in a process of continuous learning. Three steps are significant in achieving personal learning:

STEP 1:   EXPLORING THE PRESENT

The present situation must be explored as thoroughly as possible. All the factors involved – both rational and irrational, positive and negative – should be looked at. This is demanding, but not impossible. Although we tend to see the world and ourselves only from one point of view, others can give us information about ourselves, thereby challenging our assumptions. All this helps us to explore the present more fully.

STEP 2:   VISIONING THE FUTURE

Unless one is to drift from situation to situation at the mercy of circumstance, one must have personal aims and objectives that are clear expressions of one's desires and needs. A 'vision of the future' is a very important tool for assisting personal change. It provides motivation and increases the will to succeed. Without aims, people cannot bring their tenacity, drive and creativity into play. The absence of genuine desire to achieve an aim undermines individual development.

As people explore their aims and wishes, they also should spend time identifying and considering their options. Managers can devote a great deal of attention to examining business development needs without realizing that it makes sense to apply the same level of concern to personal ambitions.

STEP 3:   BRIDGING THE GAP

The third part of the process of change bridges the gap between the present situation and what the person wishes to achieve. After goals and targets are defined, resources need to be identified and allocated. The importance and difficulty of the planned change govern the quantity and quality of the resources that need to be mobilized. Large tasks require significant effort, and, as every manager knows, there is a greater risk of failure when one embarks on a programme of change with insufficient resources.

Today, more than ever, managers need the skills to manage change. These can be categorized under four headings:

1. Preparing to manage change:

    *   The skills of tracking environmental, social, political, economic, technological and industrial forces for change.
    *   The skills of conceptualizing external changes and detecting meaningful patterns.

2. Articulating choices:

    *   The skills of predicting the likely flow of changes and detecting both opportunities and threats – scenarios of what might happen.
    *   The skills of exploring possible future strategies.

3. Visioning the future:

    *   The skills of auditing one's own organization in order to determine current strengths and weaknesses.
    *   The skills of developing a vision of the future which will provide a template to guide the transformation of the organization.

4. Implementing change programmes:

    *   The skills of planning effective change programmes.
    *   The skills of leading and implementing change programmes.

Developing skills to manage change

A great change in methods of management training has been brought about through the realization that people learn better through first-hand experience. This approach, called 'experiential', has revolutionized the process of learning. The trainee ceases to be a passive recipient of lectures but a participant in action, experiment and review. Through 'experiences' trainees are able to question their current attitude, stances, skills and habits. A second realization that has changed how managers learn is the move away from an emphasis on knowledge and skills to an emphasis on developing competency – the underlying capability to perform to a high standard.

Every individual has to take a measure of responsibility for personal learning and development but continuous learning is the cornerstone of success. Successful organizations can help by creating learning opportunities, often concentrating on competencies and using experiential learning techniques. Structured activities are the most readily available way to use experiential learning approaches.

Over the years the authors have devised hundreds of structured activities, many of which are referred to in the 'Guide to Further Resources' at the end of this volume. This latest collection of activities targets improving managerial competencies. Whilst the activities can be used individually in this way, the collection also complements and extends our book *The New Unblocked Manager*, which explains in detail our Model of Managerial Competency. In *The New Unblocked Manager* we convey the 'thinking' of exceptionally proficient managers to a wider audience and in this present volume we collect together structured activities which offer learning opportunities for managers who want to translate theory into improved personal competencies. Both books are based on our definition of managerial competencies – the skills and attributes which managers need to perform their role satisfactorily. These competencies are described in *The New Unblocked Manager* and summary definitions are given in Chapter 1 of this manual. Judging from the feedback we receive, the warm reviews, the continuing sales and the fact that *The Unblocked Manager* (as the original edition was called) has been published in ten languages, managers find our approach both practical and useful.

Part I
Developing managerial competencies

1 Managerial competencies and managerial blockages

What makes a 'good' manager? At first sight there are no hard and fast rules. A manager of a rock and roll band needs different capabilities from a supervisor in a hospice. Managing in Johannesburg is different from managing in Silicon Valley. Controlling a water treatment plant in Madras poses different problems from steering General Motors through the 21st century.

Yet, despite its diverse forms, management is a craft which depends on a common basis of acquired skills, particular mind-sets and appropriate attitudes. We call these competencies. Managers learn their craft from 'masters' who blend science with art, rationality with informed intuition, accumulated experience with openness to change.

We have identified twelve domains which can be used by managers to assist their personal growth.

1. **Self-management**

   Individual managers face increasing demands. Pressure, uncertainty and complexity can demoralize and provoke psychological stress. There must be constant attention to personal well-being, efficiency and time management.

2. **Personal values**

   As the world becomes more complex, so values and beliefs are thrown into question. Ethical considerations are much more prominent than they were. Criteria for assessing what is good and bad, right or wrong, are increasingly uncertain. But managers need a positive attitude and clear principles. These can only be achieved by clarifying personal values.

3. **Leadership**

   The task of management includes leadership. No longer are administrative and organizational skills sufficient. A manager needs vision, courage, persuasiveness and enthusiasm.

4. **Creativity**

   Since ever fewer organizations are untouched by fundamental change, the management job has become increasingly creative and innovative. Transformational change and continuous improvement are expected even in the most mundane activities.

5. **Personal development**

   The management task is not external to the individual; personal development must be directed and managed. Emotions, attitudes and commitment are as important as mind-sets, conceptual tools and skills. Everyone needs a personal strategy for continuous learning.

6. **Problem solving and decision making**

   As routine tasks are automated, so the manager must operate increasingly in the domain of the non-routine. He or she can learn the skills of identifying and solving problems, and improve judgement as an aid to decision making. Without these capabilities the manager is fundamentally flawed.

7. **Objective setting**

   Determination and commitment are the principal tools of management. Without clear goals, distinct choices and challenging objectives, organizational energy is squandered. Managers need to take great care when and where they commit resources.

8. **Management style**

   The management task is always connected with shaping the behaviour of others. Managers must adopt a style which engages employees, concentrates energy, develops standards, exercises appropriate control and strives for innovation.

9. **Resource management**

   It is a cliché that the 'task of management is organizing people to get things done'. Yet the development and integration of resources continues to challenge managers, especially as knowledge has become one of the most significant resources. The task is always to achieve better results with fewer resources as the downward pressure on costs continues.

10. **Team development**

    Increasingly people are working in teams, with collective responsibility for achievement. Teamwork must be effective, stressing proper allocation of tasks, control, co-ordination and communication. The manager must become skilled at leading groups through all the trials and tribulations of development so that they emerge as resourceful and dedicated teams.

11. **People development**

The best managers develop people's latent abilities. No longer can the manager regard human assets as fixed and immutable. Good managers believe that everyone has latent abilities, and become coaches, trainers, developers and educators, as an integral part of their managerial role.

12. **Customer focus**

Every person working in a firm has 'customers' – people who use their goods or services. Sometimes these are external but often customers are internal. An approach which identifies customer needs and provides wanted goods and services is vital.

Managerial blockages

We define a *blockage* as 'a factor which inhibits the potential and output of a system. This system may be a total organization, a work team or an individual.'

Blockages are best understood by imagining a plumbing system. When blockages occur in plumbing systems they inhibit or prevent the working of the whole system and often they are difficult to trace and remedy. The plumber's task is not to concentrate on those parts of the system which are working, but to find the blockage and clear it.

For many years educators have not followed the philosophy of the plumber: they have believed in building on strengths. While this has merit, in our approach we adopt the opposite view. If the manager is a good team builder but a poor problem solver, we argue that he or she should concentrate on his or her problem-solving skills rather than hone an already sharp skill as a team builder. The blockage concept's motto is 'find those things that are holding you back, overcome your negative feelings and remove the blockages'.

All managers have the potential to develop and expand their effectiveness. The fastest and most economical way to bring about rapid self-development is to explore, understand and overcome blockages which are inhibiting success and personal growth.

It makes sense to concentrate attention on factors that are inhibiting the full achievement of potential. The twelve blockages which we use as our framework offer a vehicle for self-assessment and action planning. The categories are not meant to be complete (they relate to generic self-management skills rather than technical disciplines) but they apply widely, and the new definitions have evolved from the views of thousands of managers who have used our approach over 20 years.

The unblocked manager competency model

We assert that managers must have the following competencies:

1. Competent self-management.
2. Sound personal values.
3. Impressive leadership vision.
4. High creativity.
5. An active view of self-development.
6. A structured approach to problem solving and decision making.
7. An effective process for objective setting.
8. A positive management style.
9. Good organizing skills.
10. Strong team-development capability.
11. A dynamic approach to people development.
12. A strong customer focus.

The 'blockages' which arise from a lack of these competencies are:

1. **Incompetent self-management**
   Being unable to make the most of one's time, energy and skills; being unable to cope with the stresses of managerial life.

2. **Negative personal values**
   Being unclear about one's own values; having values that are inappropriate to leading and managing an organization. Not seeking to be a reasonable manager.

3. **Inferior leadership vision**
   Not having a coherent vision of what should be done. Being unable to engage others in the realization of a vision.

4. **Low creativity**
   Lacking the capacity to generate new ideas, failing to capitalize on ideas and lacking innovation skills.

5. **Passive personal development**
   Taking a passive attitude to the development of competency and neglecting personal development.

6. **Unstructured problem solving**
   Lacking effective strategies for problem solving and decision making.

7.   **Unclear goals**
     Lacking a goal-oriented approach to management and lacking the ability to focus energy on the achievement of specific objectives.

8.   **Negative management style**
     Being ineffective in motivating, supporting and directing people.

9.   **Poor organizing skills**
     Lacking the capacity to find, organize, exploit and use resources effectively.

10. **Weak team building capacity**
     Ineffective at integrating individuals into high-performing teams.

11. **Inactive people development**
     Lacking the ability or willingness to help others to grow and expand their capabilities.

12. **Weak customer focus**
     Not adopting a vigorous customer-oriented approach.

Each of the activities in this collection is concerned primarily with one of these blockages. There are 36 activities – three for each of the twelve blockages. Some activities are also relevant to other blockages. The Index to activities on page 33 shows which activities relate to which blockages.

To help managers to identify their own blockages, a Blockage survey is included at the end of Part I (see pages 21–30). This is reproduced from *The New Unblocked Manager*, which contains a detailed explanation of each blockage.

2 Using activities to develop managerial competencies

This chapter is designed as an introduction to the use of structured activities.

Each of the activities in this manual has been tested and developed so that the manager or facilitator can use it with confidence. Most have a theory base and are capable of providing a solid framework for analysis and debate.

It is important to distinguish between training and education. The trainer is concerned with developing specific capabilities relevant to enhanced job performance. The effective trainer designs learning events based on the latest research on adult learning. The educator is concerned with developing general capabilities which can be used in many different contexts.

Adults and children learn in different ways. The main differences are:

- Adults' minds are already filled with mental maps which guide their lives. These may act as blockages to development.

- Adults have a tremendous reservoir of accumulated knowledge which they may not know how to use.

- Adults have responsibilities and respond well to training which is directly relevant to their jobs.

- Adults (especially managers) have their own learning objectives and may direct their own learning.

- Adults see learning within the context of their broader life ambitions.

- Adults are (generally) more interested in practical techniques than broad conceptual inputs.

- Adults are more likely 'to have heard it all before' (or feel that they have). This creates resistance to learning.

- Adults (especially managers) are bound by responsibilities and accountabilities which structure much of their lives – they have less perceived freedom.

Adult learning is, therefore, a distinctive activity and the trainer would be well advised to become familiar with those values and learning technologies which are effective with people whose ages may range from 17 to 80 years!

Learning styles

Just as adults learn in distinctive ways, so do managers, and facilitators can often gain by understanding how each manager prefers to learn. Several useful typologies of learning styles have been developed.

The model we have developed to accompany the Unblocked Manager Model has eight learning styles.

EIGHT LEARNING STYLES

1. FEEDBACK
   You learn by gaining honest feedback from others about your behaviour. You need to know how others react to your way of operating. You listen to others and change your self-perception in the light of their viewpoints.

2. DISCIPLINE
   You learn by submitting yourself to disciplines and benefit from having structured approaches, checklists, and external organization. Once you have learned how to approach a situation, you follow established procedures.

3. CONCEPTUALIZING
   You learn from using a conceptual framework to simplify complexity. Once you understand basic principles, you gain confidence and feel able to 'distinguish the wood from the trees'. Your method of learning is intellectually challenging and you see theory as a vital guide to action.

4. EXPERIMENT
   You learn from trying new ways of tackling old problems. You like to try non-traditional methods and take care to review your experience. You are willing to take risks. 'Trial and error' describes your learning style.

5. ACHIEVEMENT
   You learn from undertaking challenge and overcoming real difficulties. Discovering that you can achieve provides confidence, insight, and new skills. You accept new assignments without knowing how you will cope; you learn as you progress. The real world is your teacher.

6. FAILURE

   You learn by making errors and reviewing how you failed. The experience of things going wrong provides insight into your own inadequacy. Although this may cause you emotional distress, you overcome the setbacks and identify how you behaved inappropriately. This gives you the raw material to avoid the same situation in the future. You learn by recognizing and overcoming inadequacy.

7. RECOGNITION

   You learn from being accepted by others and receiving their approval. The support of others gives you strength and reinforces your self-image. You look to others to evaluate strengths and weaknesses.

8. INSPIRATION

   You learn by inspiration from competing experienced practitioners. Watching how they operate provides you with alternative models. Observing the styles of others gives you a variety of choices and you can emulate the best practice you see.

As learning styles differ, not all trainees require the same form of training programme. In any group there are likely to be individuals with different learning profiles. The facilitator needs to design learning events with a range of learning technologies to increase the probability that all participants will benefit.

The learning organization

Most management training takes place within organizations and plays a unique role in energizing and aligning managers behind a coherent strategy. Over the last few years, we have seen the pace of change gather momentum: certainties have become conditional; competition has grown in intensity; new products and services have been developed and marketed with ever shorter lead times; and the world has increasingly become a 'global village'. In order to cope with the change from (relative) stability to today's volatile and threatening environments, managers have conceptualized their companies as 'learning organizations'. A learning organization has well-developed channels for communicating with the outside world and has found ways to tap the reservoir of ideas and insights which exist amongst employees at every level. Learning is institutionalized and provides the dynamic force needed to remain competitive and relevant. Training used to be seen as a virtuous but incidental activity. Now it is the core of strategic success in innovative organizations.

Training is an ongoing activity not confined to the classroom. A mother trains her child to tie his shoe laces. A manager trains a new recruit to answer the telephone with care. A doctor trains a patient to cope with stress. Training happens in myriad ways.

Consider the example of a mother teaching a child to tie his shoe laces. She can say 'Come here, I'll do it for you' (which teaches dependency) or she can say 'Tie your shoe lace, and tell me what you are doing so I can help' (which teaches openness and autonomy). It is this second stance which reflects the approach advocated in this guide, so well captured by the ancient Chinese saying, 'Give a man a fish and he can eat for three days. Teach the man to fish and he can eat for the rest of his life.'

It is useful to describe briefly the multiple roles of the facilitator:

- **Leader:** clarifying what should be done and attracting others to follow.

- **Follower:** seeing the learning difficulties that others have and responding to their needs.

- **Counsellor:** helping others to determine their own learning objectives and the ways in which they learn best.

- **Coach:** managing the learning process over time and introducing experiences to ensure the build-up of skills.

Added-value training

Of course, training costs money – both directly and indirectly – and particularly so with management training because not only are managers an expensive resource, but their temporary absence from the job can create other costs. Training must be seen as a way of adding value and making the best of valuable assets. The fundamental aim of organization-sponsored training cannot be learning for its own sake. Training must be seen within the economic constraints of the organization. This means that the facilitator should be adding value and generating wealth (in both economic and social terms) as an integral part of the development of the organization, not as part of a reactive support system.

To determine how the facilitator can add value, one of the questions that must be answered is 'Who is the client?'. The answer can be multiple. Certainly the trainee is a client, but the management group, the organization's strategy and its well-being are also 'clients' to be taken into account when clarifying the facilitator's role.

All too often training initiatives are remote from strategic goals. The facilitator should always be clear about organizational objectives. It is usually the organization which picks up the bill for training programmes, so their objectives need to be explicitly related to the strategic goals of the organization. Consider, for example, the professional staff in a hospital that is striving to become a leader in the treatment of burns: training inputs should be related to acquiring world-class capability in this specialized field. In a fast food outlet there are very different requirements: discipline, hygiene, team spirit and basic skills need to be developed.

Not all training is related to the development of skills. Often value is added by developing attitudes. For example, facilitators in the police force have to inculcate a set of values that will protect the citizen from inappropriate use of the power vested in police officers. Likewise a social worker needs to develop a stance towards his or her profession that permits creative and caring individual initiatives to be undertaken within a clear definition of the appropriate role. The facilitator adds value by developing the whole person.

The role of the facilitator is distinct from that of the trainer. In a sense facilitation is a sub-set of trainer skills. Although the differences are not absolute, it is helpful to consider them:

Typical trainer roles	Typical facilitator roles
Director	Enabler
Content-driven	Experience-driven
Dominant	Responsive
Controller	Empowerer
Teller	Questioner
Shaper	Provoker
Subject-centred	Client-centred
Expert	Coach

Trainers who wish to use structured activities should seek to develop a comprehensive set of skills appropriate to the typical facilitator roles mentioned. Perhaps the most important quality of a good facilitator is being 'client-centred'. This means being concerned with the internal processes and learning styles of each participant. The focus is on the learner rather than the subject area.

Ground rules

Some structured activities require participants to be prepared for criticism. They should be willing to enter into the process, explore whatever happens and question their behaviour. Facilitators are well advised not to accept contracts where participants have hostile feelings.

Ground rules have been developed by many facilitators over decades of experience. We find the following valuable in most situations:

● Find a comfortable room for the event with sufficient break-out areas for small discussions.

- Allow ample time for the activity and for discussion.

- Design instrumentation sessions into an overall learning framework.

- Create an open, relaxed but serious atmosphere.

- Avoid adopting an autocratic or domineering style.

- Be explicit about the objectives of each session and about success criteria.

- Agree a contract with participants which shapes mutual expectations.

- Carefully watch participating behaviour and re-design if necessary.

- Model behaviours that you wish to encourage.

- Deal with 'difficult' participants as early as possible.

- Have sufficient numbers of trained facilitators to provide appropriate support to individuals.

The facilitator will want to design training events as integrated sets of activities which relate to the achievement of individual and organizational objectives. This means that the overall design is critical, yet facilitators will want to have a degree of freedom to adapt their plans in the light of the flow of energy in the training group. The most significant task is the development of flexible organic structured learning designs with an appropriate degree of predictability. Effective training involves:

- Capacity to tune into organizational team and individual needs and develop these into clearly stated objectives.

- Skills in designing learning events with a balanced blend of varied activities for participants to experience.

- Capacity to develop an effective learning climate – open, positive, workmanlike and enquiring.

- Willingness to listen to and observe group members so as to determine whether to amend plans.

- Ability to explain the rationale for an event so that participants understand the concept.

- Ability to develop teamwork with other trainers, involving them in decision making and using varied experience and creativity to best advantage.

- Ability to adapt instruments, tasks and assignments to the needs of the organization and/or its members.

- Ability to help people to generalize from their experience and develop broad 'lessons' from their insights.

14

- Ability to generate the 'right' amount of fun and excitement.

- Capacity to manage the pace of learning so that people are neither bored nor overwhelmed.

- Awareness that people sometimes become distressed during experiential sessions and require help, counselling, or other forms of guidance.

- Commitment to transferring learning from the training room to 'real life'.

These preconditions are significant because they build a receptivity to learning. Even minor irritations can divert attention and reduce the learning potential of a training event. Moreover, the demonstrated ability to deal with details shows a degree of care and a 'service orientation'. This is both pleasing and confidence-building from the participants' viewpoint.

Facilitators must take their own medicine! With long work hours and travel times, they run the risk of becoming tired and unwilling to pay attention to the event. The quality of a training session is greatly influenced by the freshness, energy level and openness of the facilitator.

Introducing training events

The way in which a training event is introduced greatly affects its outcome. We favour a positive, full and open explanation of the objectives and ground rules. The facilitator's style – including manner and body language – is significant. The following checklist may be helpful:

- Clarify the objectives of the activity and success measures.

- Clarify the ground rules or constraints which affect any part of the activity.

- Define the roles of team members, teams, facilitators and any other people present.

- Link the current section of the training event with any previous activities and future activities so that the training event is seen as a coherent whole.

- Deal with questions about learning objectives and ground rules.

- If appropriate, open participants' minds to innovative ways of undertaking the task.

Facilitators often make relatively straightforward errors when designing interventions. The following list incorporates a great many of the learning points that facilitators have shared with us over the years.

THINGS TO DO

- Find ways of making the event memorable (either through a dramatic experience or a gift).

- Relate to participants as individuals – not as a group. Try to get to know as many people as possible.

- Create the right environment – open, businesslike and enquiring.

- Create a positive climate; give confidence and encouragement.

- Be explicit about your assumptions – and question them. (Practise what you preach.)

- Be willing to say 'I don't know'. Don't assume a superior attitude.

- Collect only relevant data. (Don't waste people's time.)

- Experience activities and sessions yourself before facilitating them. (Get the inside view.)

- Provide a 'road map' for the event (so that participants feel that they know where they are going).

- Maintain an appropriate level of control of the process: be 'in charge'.

- Establish success criteria (participating wherever possible) and publish these.

- Re-energize the process when commitment flags. (Have a stock of energizing activities.)

- Respect participants. (Recognize that development is basically self-regulated; recognize 'feelings'.)

- Be flexible: adapt to individuals.

- Set up mechanisms to monitor progress assessment. (Questionnaires are useful.)

- Move towards action planning – ensure that learning gets used.

- Give confident direction and short but cogent inputs. (Explain relevant theory.)

- Monitor the effectiveness of your interventions and review to improve. Learn from the experience of other facilitators.

THINGS TO AVOID

- Treating people as machines (respect everyone's feelings).

- Overwhelming people with too much at once (pace your interventions).

- Skimping on time required for processing experiences (allow time to consolidate).

- Leaving people with anxieties or uncertainties (people should leave sessions 'feeling good').

- Adopting a 'parent–child' stance (avoid talking down to people).

- Generating fear or anxiety (fear generates defensive measures and inhibits learning).

Designing workshops which use structured activities

If the members of the group are not acquainted, the facilitator should begin the workshop with one or more activities which build trust and establish rapport.

Everything that the facilitator does is significant. The quality of the experience for participants is greatly affected by the facilitator's verbal and non-verbal communication – not just during the training session or workshop but from the moment participants are informed of the event through to post-workshop care. The facilitator can do no better than adopt the principles of total quality management (TQM) throughout.

The following notes may help:

1. The initial presentation of the objectives and methods should be comprehensive and realistic. Neither grandiose promises nor over-simplifications should be allowed. Right from the beginning the prospective participant should be treated as an adult.

2. There should be the opportunity for prospective participants to discuss matters with the facilitator before committing themselves to join the workshop. At this stage the facilitator should take great care not to place any moral or other pressure on prospective participants.

3. There should be a 'contract' – which may be written or oral – between the facilitator and the participant, spelling out what each expects of the other – not just what the participant expects to gain, but also what the participant needs to contribute (attention, openness and so on). The contract should also deal with the issue of confidentiality. It is recommended that all the work undertaken in a personal development workshop should be regarded as confidential; no reports should be made to the participant's organization.

4. Deciding how many participants can be involved in a single session is important, especially where the content of the session concerns the individual. Although large groups can be broken down into sub-groups for discussions, the facilitator has to keep alert to the possibility that someone may be upset or distressed by the experience. This means that

a facilitator-to-participant ratio needs to be set. The ratio that the authors work to is usually 1:10.

5. Each training initiative requires a minimum time. Allowing insufficient time to absorb the data, conceptualize ideas and feel the impact of what has been learned, leads to an unsatisfactory or, worse, a frustrating learning experience; participants are 'left in a difficult place'. Adequate time must be allowed for the slowest members of the group to process their experiences.

6. The physical setting chosen for a training event conveys many subtle messages. There are the obvious issues like acoustics and comfortable seating, but the general impression conveyed by the venue is more significant. It should be welcoming and comfortable – never intimidating.

7. Sometimes a participant on a personal development workshop can feel considerably disturbed by the process. In these cases counselling is required. We believe that it is not advisable for any facilitator to undertake a personal development workshop unless there is adequate provision for detecting and helping anyone who may be a 'casualty' from the experience. Counselling is a learned skill, so the counsellors need to be qualified and have sufficient time to undertake the workload generated.

8. The facilitator should adopt a style that is compassionate and developmental. High-energy and extremely confrontational styles are not recommended.

9. No workshop is complete without part of the session being devoted to 'back home' application of the insights and learning points.

10. It is wise to follow up workshops. Two benefits of a structured review are that review data provide the raw material for improvement and that any undetected 'casualties' will come to light and can be given counselling.

Practical considerations

Before facilitating a training session it is useful to run through a checklist to see that all practical considerations have been taken into account. These are the important points:

ROOM SIZE AND VENUE

- Is the room large enough?
- Are the chairs comfortable?

- Can everyone see the trainer and the visual aids?

- Is the room sufficiently quiet?

- Are there provisions for break-out conversations?

COMFORT LEVELS

- Are toilet arrangements adequate?

- Are there supplies of water and other refreshments?

- Is the air conditioning satisfactory?

- Does the room feel light and airy?

AUDIO/VISUAL AIDS

- Is there a serviceable overhead projector?

- Are visual aids clear and attractive?

- Have trainer's notes been prepared?

- Has the presentation been synchronized with audio/visual aids?

- Do visual aids make an amusing or vivid impact?

HANDOUTS AND INSTRUMENTATION

- Have sufficient copies been prepared?

- Are handouts conveniently packaged?

- Are handouts available for each session?

- Has any necessary preparatory work been completed?

Action planning

Rarely should a facilitator contemplate concluding an experiential learning event without an action planning session. The purpose of action planning is to focus attention on the implications and utilization of learning. In essence the action planning session answers the question 'So what?'.

Action planning, preferably supported by on-the-job coaching, is an essential ingredient in the learning process. Research into training effectiveness indicates that the more 'real' the problem the more effective will be the learning. It has been shown that generic learning tends to be valuable only when the skills learned are put to use in practical situations.

The purpose of action planning is clear, but the process is often mishandled. These are the common hazards:

- *Rushed planning* results in superficial task allocation and control, and lack of co-ordinated action.

- *Forced pace* results in participants being pressured to come to premature conclusions, inadequate decision making and ineffectual action.

- *Lack of sharing* results in participants avoiding public debate of their plans, so a consensus about ends and means fails to develop.

- *Low feedback* results in unrealistic assessment of the situation and opportunities.

- *Lack of review* results in ineffective identification of success criteria and inadequate monitoring of results.

- *Lack of specificity* results in action plans that are vague or confused.

- *'Political' naivety* results in action plans that are impossible to implement.

In general we recommend that facilitators should allocate between 10 and 20 per cent of available time to action planning. This should be positioned at the end of the session and be the last component of the event. The following guidelines will enable facilitators to help participants develop effective action plans:

- Help participants to transform their proposals into a coherent project plan.

- Help participants to describe, in depth, their present situation and explore all the forces which are relevant.

- Help participants to clarify what they feel that they want to change and why.

- Help participants to feel strong about their capacity to effect change.

- Help participants to visualize what the situation will be like when they have achieved their personal objectives.

- Help participants to set themselves tasks that are measurable.

- Help participants to prepare for both expected and unexpected difficulties.

- Help participants to identify the stakeholders in the change process and decide how to handle each person.

The blockage survey

This survey helps individuals to identify their managerial strengths and weaknesses using The Unblocked Manager Competencies Model. It offers a framework for systematically assessing personal strengths and blockages to managing effectively.

The survey takes approximately 20 minutes to complete, followed by 40 minutes for reflection or discussion.

Method

1. Read the instructions before you complete the survey.
2. Try to consider each statement separately and leave analysis until the end of the survey.
3. When you have completed the survey, consider the results carefully in order to assess how valid they are for you.

A note of caution

Although the survey is methodical and logical, it reflects your subjective views and it should therefore be seen as an aid to self-review rather than as a scientific measure.

Reproduced from *Developing Your People: Easy-to-use activities for improving management skills* by Mike Woodcock and Dave Francis, Gower, Aldershot

Instructions for completing the survey

This survey will help you to clarify your own development needs.
As you score the questionnaire reflect on:

- Your current abilities compared with excellent performers in jobs similar to yours.

- The new competencies that your job will require in three years' time.

- Capabilities that you need for your career plan.

On the following pages you will find five sections. Complete each section in the same way.

For each section you have 20 points which *must* be allocated. Look over the list of 12 items and allocate the points to represent your personal development needs. One item can receive all 20 points, or you can spread the points over as many items as you wish – the aim is to highlight your own development needs.

Reproduced from *Developing Your People: Easy-to-use activities for improving management skills* by Mike Woodcock and Dave Francis, Gower, Aldershot

Section one

Allocate 20 points between these 12 items:

In my job, I need to do these things more or better ...

1. Maintain a high level of personal energy.   ☐

2. Know where I stand on matters of principle.   ☐

3. Have a clear 'vision' of what needs to be done.   ☐

4. Provide creative ideas.   ☐

5. Take my own development seriously.   ☐

6. Solve problems in a structured way.   ☐

7. Set clear goals for others.   ☐

8. Motivate those who work for me.   ☐

9. Manage projects efficiently.   ☐

10. Build high-performing teams.   ☐

11. Create opportunities to help others to develop.   ☐

12. Focus on satisfying customers (internal or external).   ☐

Reproduced from *Developing Your People: Easy-to-use activities for improving management skills* by Mike Woodcock and Dave Francis, Gower, Aldershot

Section two

Allocate 20 points between these 12 items:

I need to improve these activities ...

13. Seeking outside assessments of my group's efficiency. ☐

14. Holding regular coaching sessions with my staff. ☐

15. Leading teams towards achieving shared objectives. ☐

16. Making better use of available resources. ☐

17. Taking a firm line with low-performing people. ☐

18. Running productive meetings. ☐

19. Developing a wider range of options before taking a decision. ☐

20. Setting time aside for my own learning. ☐

21. Suggesting radical ways to improve processes. ☐

22. Obtaining other people's commitment to objectives. ☐

23. Dealing confidently with decisions that involve finely balanced value judgements. ☐

24. Managing my own time efficiently. ☐

Section three

Allocate 20 points between these 12 items:

I would perform better if I …

25. Reduced my personal stress level.

26. Operated from a coherent 'philosophy' of management.

27. Enrolled others to support my initiatives.

28. Suggested more innovate ideas.

29. Set demanding development objectives for myself.

30. Took more time for decision making when issues are important.

31. Measured other people's performance objectively.

32. Gave greater emotional support to others.

33. Delegated effectively.

34. Developed a more positive climate in teams.

35. Gave counselling to my staff.

36. Worked co-operatively with other departments and teams.

Section four

Allocate 20 points between these 12 items:

I would be a more skilful manager if I ...

37. Sought regular feedback about performance from internal or external customers.

38. Actively provided opportunities for staff to develop their abilities.

39. Helped work groups to clarify their team development needs.

40. Designed effective work processes.

41. Communicated systematically to my staff.

42. Ensured that key objectives were measured.

43. Consciously involved others in decision making.

44. Tried new ideas to extend my experience.

45. Seized opportunities that others miss.

46. Enrolled others in my vision of what needs to be done.

47. Fundamentally questioned my own values from time to time.

48. Dealt with setbacks without losing confidence.

Section five

Allocate 20 points between these 12 items:

My own development needs are to...

49. Maintain a higher level of energy. ☐

50. Behave in ways that are more consistent with my beliefs. ☐

51. Be more assertive. ☐

52. Maintain effort when solutions cannot be readily found. ☐

53. Learn from honest feedback on my own strengths and weaknesses. ☐

54. Handle complex information with clarity and confidence. ☐

55. Monitor progress towards the achievement of goals. ☐

56. Supervise others according to their individual needs. ☐

57. Organize people and resources efficiently. ☐

58. Develop high-performing teams. ☐

59. Appraise comprehensively the performance of subordinates. ☐

60. Develop a clear understanding of my (internal or external) customers' needs. ☐

Reproduced from *Developing Your People: Easy-to-use activities for improving management skills*
by Mike Woodcock and Dave Francis, Gower, Aldershot

Answer grid for the blockage survey

Copy the number for each of the five sections onto the answer grid below and add the scores for each horizontal line.

TOTALS

1	24	25	48	49		
						1
2	23	26	47	50		
						2
3	22	27	46	51		
						3
4	21	28	45	52		
						4
5	20	29	44	53		
						5
6	19	30	43	54		
						6
7	18	31	42	55		
						7
8	17	32	41	56		
						8
9	16	33	40	57		
						9
10	15	34	39	58		
						10
11	14	35	38	59		
						11
12	13	36	37	60		
						12

Now transfer the numbers to the next page.

Scoring sheet for the blockage survey

Instructions

1. Enter the grand total from the answer grid sheet for each of the 12 categories in the *Your score* column.
2. Fill in the *Ranking* column by giving your highest score a ranking of 1, the second highest score a ranking of 2 and continue. Your lowest score is ranked 12.

	YOUR SCORE	RANKING	BLOCKAGE
1			Incompetent self-management
2			Negative personal values
3			Inferior leadership vision
4			Low creativity
5			Passive personal development
6			Unstructured problem solving and decision making
7			Unclear goals
8			Negative management style
9			Poor organizing skills
10			Weak team-building capacity
11			Inactive people development
12			Weak customer focus

What do the scores mean?

Your highest scores represent possible blockages. We suggest that you take the three or four highest scores and explore them further, possibly using the relevant activities in this manual.

Reproduced from *Developing Your People: Easy-to-use activities for improving management skills*
by Mike Woodcock and Dave Francis, Gower, Aldershot

Part II
The activities

Index to activities

A = PRIMARY FOCUS
B = SECONDARY FOCUS

ACTIVITY

1. Self-assessment questionnaire
2. Time management workshop
3. Assess your stress level
4. Exploring personal values
5. Managerial values questionnaire
6. Cave rescue
7. Boot camp
8. Manager's audit of communication effectiveness (MACE)
9. A personal skills inventory
10. Unlocking creativity
11. Personal paradigms questionnaire
12. Blu cross
13. Learning styles questionnaire
14. Golden Sunshine Resort: a case study in management development
15. Personal visioning questionnaire
16. Stakeholder analysis
17. Problem solving using Force Field Analysis
18. 'If you don't measure it you are only practising'

Weakness	1	2	3	4	5	6	7	8	9	10	11	12	13	14	15	16	17	18
Weak customer focus							B									B		
Inactive people development													B	B				
Weak team-building capacity						B	B					B		B		B		B
Poor organizing skills											B							
Negative management styles	B			B	B			B			B				B			
Unclear goals						B	B							B	B			
Unstructured problem solving						B				B						A	A	A
Passive personal development	B	B			B				B				A	A	A			
Low creativity		B	B							A	A	A						
Inferior leadership vision			B			A		A	A	B								
Negative personal values				A	A	A		B			B		B			A	A	A
Incompetent self-management	A	A	A						B									B

33

Index to activities

A = PRIMARY FOCUS
B = SECONDARY FOCUS

ACTIVITY	Weak customer focus	Inactive people development	Weak team-building capacity	Poor organizing skills	Negative management styles	Unclear goals	Unstructured problem solving	Passive personal development	Low creativity	Inferior leadership vision	Negative personal values	Incompetent self-management
19 Tiers of objectives			B			A					B	
20 Team visioning			B			A						
21 'Boom' objectives		B				A	B					
22 The failure workbook	B				A		B			B		
23 Theory X – Theory Y: the essence of management					A					B	B	
24 Leadership review				B	A					B		
25 Innovative leader questionnaire				A					B			
26 Cozibears: a case study in organizational design	B		B	A		B						
27 Situational management				A	B					B		
28 Team communication: the whisper chain			A				B					
29 Team feedback			A	B	B							
30 Intergroup efficiency	B	B	A	B								
31 Coaching workbook		A						B				
32 Tools for developing managers		A						B				
33 Development review process		A					B	B				
34 Customer orientation index	A									B		
35 Customer decision process analysis	A					B				B		
36 Internal customer survey workbook	A									B		

34

Symbols

 Handout sheet

 OHP transparency master

 Task sheet

1

Self-assessment questionnaire

Objectives

- To define 'self-management'.
- To clarify existing competency in self-management.
- To establish a personal action plan.
- To strengthen self-management.

Group size

1. This assessment process deals with personal issues. All participants should be volunteers.

2. It should be used with groups that have already developed a high level of openness and trust.

Time required

1 hour 25 minutes.

Materials required

1. Task sheet 1.1: Self-assessment questionnaire.

2. Task sheet 1.2: Self-assessment questionnaire: scoring and interpretation.

3.   Handout 1.1: Seven self-management challenges.

4.   Task sheet 1.3: Key discussion questions.

5.   OHP 1.1.

Description

To define and explore key personal challenges.

	Method	Approx time
1	Introduce the activity by referring to the objectives and emphasizing that the sharing of information in this session is entirely voluntary. Participants should share only the information they wish to disclose. The purpose of the activity is exploratory. The views of one participant are no more correct than those of any other.	5 mins
2	Distribute Task sheet 1.1: Self-assessment questionnaire, and ask for it to be completed by each participant as directed.	15 mins
3	Give a brief presentation on the seven challenges of self-management, using OHP 1.1.	10 mins
4	Invite participants to meet with one or two others with whom they feel comfortable. Distribute copies of Task sheet 1.2: Self-assessment questionnaire: scoring and interpretation; Handout 1.1: Seven self-management challenges; and Task sheet 1.3: Key discussion questions. Ask the small groups to complete the assignment as directed.	45 mins
5	Gather the participants together and ask each individual to share one learning point from the session. There should be no discussion of personal issues. Announce any arrangements for follow-up counselling at this point.	10 mins

Self-assessment questionnaire

Directions

Think about yourself. Read each item below and circle a number from 1 to 7 to indicate where you feel you are now with respect to that issue. Then put an X through a number to indicate where you would *like* to be on the same issue. Repeat these directions for each item.

1. Looking back over the last year, I feel that I have learned…
   Nothing that has changed my view of myself   1__2__3__4__5__6__7   Much that has changed my view of myself

2. Most of the time I feel that…
   My life is uneventful   1__2__3__4__5__6__7   Life is bursting with excitement

3. I feel that…
   No one benefits from what I do   1__2__3__4__5__6__7   People benefit greatly from what I do

4. In relation to my physical well-being…
   I am physically unfit   1__2__3__4__5__6__7   I am physically extremely fit

5. If I could change my life I would…
   Make fundamental changes   1__2__3__4__5__6__7   Make no fundamental changes

6. My close relationships with others are a source of…
   Deep dissatisfaction   1__2__3__4__5__6__7   Deep satisfaction

7. In the last year I have…
   Achieved little   1__2__3__4__5__6__7   Achieved a great deal

8. I set time aside for learning…
   Almost never   1__2__3__4__5__6__7   Very frequently

9. People would say of me that…
   I lack enthusiasm   1__2__3__4__5__6__7   I am very enthusiastic

10. I believe that in my life…
    I have contributed nothing of lasting value   1__2__3__4__5__6__7   I have contributed something of lasting value

11. When I look at myself in the mirror, I feel…
    Regret   1__2__3__4__5__6__7   Pleasure

12. I do what I really want to do...
    Almost never   1__2__3__4__5__6__7   Most of the time

13. The people who are close to me...
    Would prefer I was   1__2__3__4__5__6__7   Honour me as I am
    different

14. I am achieving...
    Nothing beyond   1__2__3__4__5__6__7   Significant new
    what I achieved before   accomplishments

15. I invest in my own learning...
    No effort   1__2__3__4__5__6__7   A great deal of effort

16. I feel excited about things...
    Almost never   1__2__3__4__5__6__7   Most of the time

17. When I look back I feel...
    Regret   1__2__3__4__5__6__7   Satisfaction

18. I am...
    Very unfit   1__2__3__4__5__6__7   Very fit

19. I spend my time as I want...
    Rarely   1__2__3__4__5__6__7   Most of the time

20. I give love...
    Never   1__2__3__4__5__6__7   Often

21. My personal objectives...
    Don't stretch me   1__2__3__4__5__6__7   Stretch me a great deal

22. My perception of myself...
    Has changed little   1__2__3__4__5__6__7   Has changed greatly
    over the past five years   over the past five years

23. I feel joyful...
    Never   1__2__3__4__5__6__7   Often

24. I derive a great deal of satisfaction from my job...
    Never   1__2__3__4__5__6__7   All of the time

25. I feel physically strong...
    Never   1__2__3__4__5__6__7   All of the time

26. I would like to change the basic aspects of my life...
    Considerably   1__2__3__4__5__6__7   Not at all

27. I have as true friends...
    No one   1__2__3__4__5__6__7   Many people

28. My career so far...
    Disappoints me   1__2__3__4__5__6__7   Delights me

40

29. I feel that next year I...
     Will learn nothing   1__2__3__4__5__6__7   Will learn important
     things

30. I feel a great curiosity towards many aspects of life...
     Never   1__2__3__4__5__6__7   Frequently

31. I believe the world is a little bit better for my being here...
     Never   1__2__3__4__5__6__7   Often

32. My weight is...
     Far too high   1__2__3__4__5__6__7   Just right

33. I do what I really want to do...
     Never   1__2__3__4__5__6__7   Most of the time

34. I receive love...
     Never   1__2__3__4__5__6__7   Often

35. The next stage of my career...
     Holds no challenge   1__2__3__4__5__6__7   Holds real challenge

Self-assessment questionnaire: scoring and interpretation

Scoring

DIRECTIONS

Review your answers to the Self-assessment questionnaire and subtract the 'where you are now' score from the 'want to be' score for each item. Record the difference for each item in the appropriate box below. Record a zero for any negative scores. Total the scores for each vertical column and write the totals in the boxes provided. When you have completed the scoring chart, transfer your scores to the interpretation chart.

	I	II	III	IV	V	VI	VII
	1	2	3	4	5	6	7
	8	9	10	11	12	13	14
	15	16	17	18	19	20	21
	22	23	24	25	26	27	28
	29	30	31	32	33	34	35
TOTALS							

T

INTERPRETATION

	Your Score	Personal Development Challenge
I		CONTINUOUS LEARNING
II		HIGH ENERGY
III		HIGH SENSE OF WORTH
IV		PHYSICAL WELL-BEING
V		HIGH AUTONOMY
VI		NOURISHING RELATIONSHIPS
VII		PROGRESSIVE ACHIEVEMENT

Self-management

The Self-assessment questionnaire helps you explore the personal challenges that you are facing. The higher your score on a challenge, the more likely it is that the particular challenge is important to you. Consider your scores and what they mean to you. Read the explanations of the Seven challenges (Handout 1.1) and then discuss the issues raised with one or two other people, making sure that you give each other sufficient time. Consolidate your thinking by answering the Key discussion questions (Task sheet 1.3).

Seven self-management challenges

Challenge one – Continuous learning

A high score indicates that you are not nourishing your learning and personal development. Continuous learning is essential for well-being. Effective self-management requires that you seek opportunities for new insights, stimulation and intellectual, spiritual and emotional development.

Challenge two – High energy

A high score indicates that you are not in contact with sources of inner energy. A sense of excitement, joy and aliveness characterizes the healthy person. Such emotions are common among children but can be lost in adult life. Effective self-management requires that the aliveness sensation is rediscovered and flows into daily behaviour.

Challenge three – High sense of worth

A high score indicates that you do not feel that you are making a significant contribution to the wider world. Everyone wants to feel that what they are doing creates some benefits outside of their own well-being. Effective self-management requires that each individual finds a sense of vocation.

Challenge four – Physical well-being

A high score indicates that you are not enjoying your physical self and feel less fit than you could. It has been shown that physical fitness has many psychological benefits. Effective self-management requires that you realize more of your physical potential, although it is not necessary to become an athlete or fitness freak.

Challenge five – High autonomy

A high score indicates that you are spending time doing things that you would prefer not to do. The reasons may be many, for example, commitments, habits or anxiety. Effective self-management requires that you increase your sense of mastery over your life and the proportion of time that you spend on the things that you want to do.

Challenge six – Nourishing relationships

A high score indicates that you lack deep and open communication with others who are close to you. Real affection requires that individuals are accepted for who they really are. Without this acceptance loneliness occurs. Effective self-management requires that you find ways to acquire the supportive, open and close communication that most of us desire.

Challenge seven – Progressive accomplishment

A high score indicates that you are not setting meaningful challenges. It is satisfying to look back on a career and see that development has been progressive. Effective self-management requires that a succession of new challenges are achieved.

Key discussion questions

Directions

Consider the explanations of the seven challenges of self-management and answer the questions below. Discuss with the members of your small group.

1. What areas for improved self-management are relevant to you?

    a)

    b)

    c)

2. Which is the most important area: a, b, or c?

Why is this important?	What could happen if you change?	How could you change your behaviour?

3. Which is the second most important area: a, b, or c?

Why is this important?	What could happen if you change?	How could you change your behaviour?

4. What forces are preventing you from changing a, b, or c?

Forces	Why these occur

5. What will you have to do differently in order to progress?
    Do more or better   Do less or stop   Start to do

The seven challenges of self-management

I   CONTINUOUS LEARNING

II   HIGH ENERGY

III   HIGH SENSE OF WORTH

IV   PHYSICAL WELL-BEING

V   HIGH AUTONOMY

VI   NOURISHING RELATIONSHIPS

VII   PROGRESSIVE ACHIEVEMENT

2

Time management workshop

Objectives

- To introduce principles of time management.
- To heighten consciousness of how time is spent.
- To provoke a review of time planning.

Group size

Any number.

Time required

- 10 minutes (first session): Preparation/data collection.
- 2 hours (second session): Workshop.

Materials required

1. Task sheet 2.1: Time log.
2. Task sheet 2.2: Time log: analysis.
3. Task sheet 2.3: Time management review.
4. Task sheet 2.4: Time management questionnaire.

5. Task sheet 2.5: Discussion task.

6. Task sheet 2.6: Time management: action planning.

7. OHP 2.1.

Description

To evaluate use of time and plan ways to improve time managment.

	Method	Approx time
1	Introduce participants to Task sheet 2.1: Time log approximately two weeks before the Time management workshop. Instruct each participant to complete the Time log and Task sheet 2.2: Time log: analysis as directed and bring the analysis to the workshop.	10 mins
2	Open the Time management workshop by outlining the objectives and structure of the session.	5 mins
3	Divide participants into groups of two or three to complete Task sheet 2.3: Time management review as directed.	30 mins
4	Task sheet 2.4: Time management questionnaire is completed as directed.	30 mins
5	Discuss the skills of an effective time manager by talking through the OHP.	10 mins
6	Participants work in their small groups on Task sheet 2.5: Discussion task.	15 mins
7	Task sheet 2.6: Time management: action planning form is completed as directed.	20 mins
8	Members of the whole group share their insights from the experiences.	10 mins

Time log

Directions

In approximately two weeks you will attend a Time Management Workshop. Please prepare for this workshop by keeping a log of how you actually spend your time. Select three days before the workshop that confront you with a time management challenge and keep a time log. Do not change your normal behaviour. Make three photocopies of the log sheets and keep records as indicated. Then complete Task sheet 2.2: Time log: analysis, as directed.

Time Log Sheet   Date _____

Time	Activities Being Undertaken	Benefits of These Activities
7.00a.m.		
7.30a.m.		
8.00a.m.		
8.30a.m.		
9.00a.m.		
9.30a.m.		
10.00a.m.		
10.30a.m.		
11.00a.m.		
11.30a.m.		
12.00 noon		

Task sheet 2.1 (page 2 of 2)

Time	Activities Being Undertaken	Benefits of These Activities
12.30p.m.		
1.00p.m.		
1.30p.m.		
2.00p.m.		
2.30p.m.		
3.00p.m.		
3.30p.m.		
4.00p.m.		
4.30p.m.		
5.00p.m.		
5.30p.m.		
6.00p.m.		
6.30p.m.		
7.00p.m.		
Later		

Time log: analysis

Directions

Take the data you have accumulated on your Time Logs and analyse them as shown in the example below. Include all of the activities and rank them in frequency order. Use your own definitions of activities. Then complete the pie chart display.

Example activity analysis

Activities	*Number of entries*	*Total*
1. Direct customer contact	JHT JHT JHT JHT III	23
2. Completing order documents	JHT JHT JHT IIII	19
3. Meetings with colleagues	JHT JHT JHT II	17
4. Training employees	JHT JHT III	13
5. Meeting with boss	JHT III	8
6. Reading reports	JHT I	6

Reproduced from *Developing Your People: Easy-to-use activities for improving management skills* by Mike Woodcock and Dave Francis, Gower, Aldershot

Directions

Draw a pie chart to display the data in graphic form as shown in the example below.

Sample chart

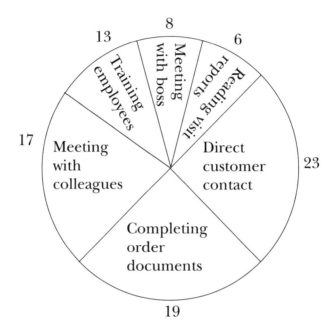

Your chart

54

Reproduced from *Developing Your People: Easy-to-use activities for improving management skills* by Mike Woodcock and Dave Francis, Gower, Aldershot

Time management review

Directions

Consider the results of your Time log and discuss the patterns that emerged with one or two other people. Then complete the statements below.

1. Most of my time is spent doing these things:

   a)

   b)

   c)

   d)

   e)

2. The activities that I believe produce the greatest benefits are:

   Activities   *Benefits*   *Time spent*

   a)

   b)

   c)

   d)

   e)

3. The activities that I believe produce the fewest benefits are:

   Activities   *Benefits*   *Time spent*

   a)

   b)

   c)

   d)

   e)

Reproduced from *Developing Your People: Easy-to-use activities for improving management skills*
by Mike Woodcock and Dave Francis, Gower, Aldershot

4. The things that prevent me (time stealers) from using my time more effectively are:

Time stealers	Why these occur	What could be done to minimize

Time management questionnaire

Directions

Respond to each item by circling the appropriate number. Then complete Task sheet 2.5 as directed.

1. I frequently review how my time is spent.

    Totally untrue   1__2__3__4__5__6__7   Totally true

2. I have full control over how I spend my time.

    Totally untrue   1__2__3__4__5__6__7   Totally true

3. I carefully plan in advance how I will spend my time.

    Totally untrue   1__2__3__4__5__6__7   Totally true

4. I keep to my time plans.

    Totally untrue   1__2__3__4__5__6__7   Totally true

5. I keep waste of time to an absolute minimum.

    Totally untrue   1__2__3__4__5__6__7   Totally true

6. I do not allow others to steal my time.

    Totally untrue   1__2__3__4__5__6__7   Totally true

7. I spend most time on achieving my key objectives.

    Totally untrue   1__2__3__4__5__6__7   Totally true

8. I insist that other people present me with concise information and proposals.

    Totally untrue   1__2__3__4__5__6__7   Totally true

9. I concentrate well on what people are saying.

    Totally untrue   1__2__3__4__5__6__7   Totally true

10. I do not allow myself to become extremely tired.

    Totally untrue   1__2__3__4__5__6__7   Totally true

11. I balance work time and leisure extremely well.

    Totally untrue   1__2__3__4__5__6__7   Totally true

12. I make ample time for activities that I really enjoy.

    Totally untrue   1__2__3__4__5__6__7   Totally true

Reproduced from *Developing Your People: Easy-to-use activities for improving management skills* by Mike Woodcock and Dave Francis, Gower, Aldershot

13.   I reallocate time according to the needs of the situation.

Totally untrue   1___2___3___4___5___6___7   Totally true

14.   I do not rush when this would reduce the quality of what I do.

Totally untrue   1___2___3___4___5___6___7   Totally true

15.   I feel capable of making substantial changes in my personal management of time.

Totally untrue   1___2___3___4___5___6___7   Totally true

Discussion task

Directions

With one or two other participants, discuss the patterns shown by your answers to the Time management style questionnaire. You should highlight aspects of time management that you wish to work on. Try to concentrate on a limited number of areas to improve. Then complete the chart below.

Topic	Need for development (high/medium /low)	What I could do	What I will do
1. Review time use			
2. Exercise control			
3. Plan time use			
4. Keep to time plans			
5. Reduce time wastage			
6. Resist time stealers			

7. Focus time use			
8. Structure time input			
9. Concentrate on others			
10. Resist tiredness			
11. Balance work and leisure			
12. Make time for enjoyment			
13. Reallocate time flexibly			
14. Avoid rushing			
15. Feel personal power			

Time management: action planning

Directions

Answer Questions 1–3 below. Then discuss Question 4 before recording your answers to that question.

1. What are your key job objectives?

    a.

    b.

    c.

    d.

    e.

2. What are your key career objectives?

    a.

    b.

    c.

3. What are your key personal objectives?

    a.

    b.

    c.

    d.

    e.

4. What should you be doing differently in order to invest your time in ways that better meet your objectives?

I should be spending more time on:	I should spending less time on:	I should change my behaviour in these ways:

THE MASTER TIME MANAGER

- KNOWS WHERE TIME IS SPENT

- SETS CLEAR PERSONAL AND WORK OBJECTIVES

- PLANS TO INVEST TIME TO MEET OBJECTIVES

- DOES NOT ALLOW OTHERS TO BECOME 'STEALERS' OF TIME

- IS PERSONALLY EFFICIENT

- DELEGATES PRUDENTLY

- DOES THINGS ONLY ONCE

- DOES THINGS WELL

- KEEPS TIME FOR LEARNING AND RELAXATION

- WATCHES HOW OTHERS SPEND TIME AND LEARNS TO IMPROVE

Reproduced from *Developing Your People: Easy-to-use activities for improving management skills*
by Mike Woodcock and Dave Francis, Gower, Aldershot

3

Assess your stress level

Objectives

- To help managers explore the causes of stress.
- To help participants determine their personal stressors.
- To contribute to action planning for stress reduction.

Group size

Any number.

Time required

1 hour and 30 minutes.

Materials required

1. Handout 3.1: Stress handout.
2. Task sheet 3.1: Stress self-counselling worksheet.
3. OHP 3.1.

Description

To explore the causes of stress and decide what can be done to reduce unhealthy levels of stress.

Method		Approx time
1	Introduce the session by giving an input on the nature of stress. This is drawn from Handout 3.1: Stress handout, and supported by OHP 3.1: Stress: 'Emotional tension'.	10 mins
2	Divide participants into pairs or trios. Each person takes turns to act as the 'Counsellor' and 'Client'. Answers to the questions are recorded on the worksheet. Each 'Client' should receive 30 minutes of counselling.	1 hour
3	Re-assemble pairs into the group. Ask each pair to share one item of learning. Arrangements for follow-up counselling should be explained at this stage.	20 mins

Stress handout

Stress is a complex topic. It affects millions of people around the world, limiting effectiveness and enjoyment of life. Stress can be defined as 'emotional tension'. It has many causes which, for the sake of simplicity, we will divide into two types. Sometimes stress is caused by injury, ill-health or medical emergency. The second cause of stress is a mismatch between what the person wants and needs and what the world has to offer.

Stress is a very personal matter. Some people suffer a stress response every time they let their cat out for the evening, whereas other people can run a large company, or even a country, without suffering undue emotional strain. There are no 'rights' or 'wrongs' – the stress response is real if it affects you.

The negative effects of stress can be divided into four categories:

1. Physical effects: There is evidence that certain illnesses are provoked by stress. Psychological pressure can have physical results. Some medical specialists claim that excessive stress over an extended period can result in life-threatening conditions. Many of the people who visit their medical practitioners are suffering from emotional tension.

2. Social effects: Stress is not a personal issue – it affects those who are close to the sufferer. One only has to spend some time with a family in which one member is suffering from stress to understand the effect on relationships. Many people find that stress is almost infectious – it heightens the emotional atmosphere in an unhealthy way.

3. Decision-making effects: Stress is directly related to a deterioration of decision-making prowess. For example, studies done on the performance of airline pilots whilst under stress demonstrate that even 'common sense' can be thrown to the winds when the pilot feels under emotional tension. Many of us suffer the same deterioration in our decision-making capability during periods of stress (although the costs of failure are, one hopes, lower).

4. Sense of well-being effects: Stress is disturbing, irritating, dulling and energy-sapping. It undermines self-confidence and takes away much of the joy of living. Those who suffer from stress often feel that life has to be 'got through' and endured. Each day is experienced as a trial. Pleasure in being alive is absent. This is deeply disappointing for the person and affects the image that others have of them.

Many people who suffer from stress feel that what they most want to do is free themselves of the negative effects – as if stress were a foreign body which has to be removed. This is not easily done. Stress is part of the person, and needs to be understood in depth before it can be vanquished. Overcoming

65

Reproduced from *Developing Your People: Easy-to-use activities for improving management skills* by Mike Woodcock and Dave Francis, Gower, Aldershot

stress results from following a path of self-discovery, coming to terms with the inner causes, and growing by learning and increasing mastery of the self. In other words, overcoming stress is the result of increased self-knowledge and there are no cheap and easy solutions.

For this reason the causes of stress need to be treated as friends rather than enemies. We need to understand those factors which make us feel the way that we do. In the exploration of stress the biggest threat is one's own attitude: once a person feels irritated or dismissive of their own stress reactions, there is little possibility of going further. The person becomes stressed about being stressed!

Stress self-counselling worksheet

Ask the questions in the left-hand column to another participant, and record their answers to the questions in the right-hand column. When all 15 questions have been answered, hand the completed questionnaire to your interviewee and discuss any patterns in the answers. The interviewee then completes the conclusion as directed.

Questions	Answers
1. Do you suffer from stress?	
2. How do you experience stress (what happens inside you)?	
3. What are the positive effects of stress for you?	
4. What are the negative effects of stress for you?	
5. In what situations do you experience stress? Give as many examples as you can.	
6. What triggers stress in you?	
7. What helps you to reduce your stress level?	

Questions	Answers
8. Do you have hopes which have not been fulfilled? What are they?	
9. How far do you feel that you are able to communicate closely with other people?	
10. What do you do that has little meaning for you?	
11. Is part of your stress connected with a feeling of obligation or duty to others? How do you experience this?	
12. To what extent do you derive pleasure from your work? Why are some elements less pleasurable?	
13. Is there a conflict between what you do and what you feel you should do? How does this affect you?	
14. What is your attitude to your own stress? How do you value it?	
15. What elements of stress could you reduce? How do you need to change in attitude and behaviour?	

Conclusion

Having considered my answers to the 15 questions, these are three things I need to change in my working life:

	WHAT TO CHANGE	REASONS WHY
1		
2		
3		

STRESS: 'EMOTIONAL TENSION'

- Widely experienced

- Experienced personally

- External stressors shape the stress response

- Negative effects:
  - health
  - social
  - decision making
  - well-being

- Reducing stress requires self-knowledge

'Make stress your friend – it's part of you!'

4

Exploring personal values

Objectives

- To assist in the definition of personal values.
- To introduce the values clarification process.
- To help participants reconsider personal values.

Group size

Any number.

Time required

2 to 3 hours.

Materials required

1. Task sheet 4.1: Values questionnaire.
2. Handout 4.1: Clarifying values.
3. Task sheet 4.2: Values clarification exercise.
4. OHP 4.1.

Description

This activity clarifies deep-seated beliefs. Ensure that all participants are volunteers.

	Method	Approx time
1	Introduce the activity by saying that it presents an opportunity to explore personal values but must be undertaken voluntarily. Hand out copies of the Values questionnaire. At this point the facilitator may suggest that anyone who is uncomfortable may decline to participate. No explanation for this decision should be requested.	5 mins
2	Ask participants to complete Task sheet 4.1: Values questionnaire.	1 hour
3	Give a short presentation on values clarification, using OHP 4.1: Clarifying personal values.	15 mins
4	Distribute copies of Handout 4.1: Clarifying values. Divide participants into pairs or groups of three and ask them to complete Task sheet 4.2: Values clarification exercise as directed.	1 hour
5	Ask all participants for their comments on the process. Learning points are shared. Invite anyone concerned by the results of the activity to speak with you privately after the session.	15 mins

Values questionnaire

Directions

Your values are what you believe to be important and worthwhile. Values provide a basis for action: a framework for personal decisions. The Values questionnaire has been developed to enable managers and others in professional jobs to clarify their values. There are no 'right' and 'wrong' answers – it is your values that define how you behave.

Individually answer each of the questions below, entering your responses in the spaces provided. Work methodically through the questionnaire. Make your answers as complete as possible and try to be totally honest.

1. My core values are ...

    Towards co-workers and staff

    Towards the customers of my organization

    Towards how I live

    Towards other people close to me

    Towards the environment

    Towards the wider community

2. When I consider my values, I feel ...

    Satisfied with these elements   Why?

73

Dissatisfied with these elements   Why?

3.   Although I believe that these values are important, at the moment I do not spend time actually pursuing them ...

Values I hold but do not pursue   Why?

4.   I do these things that I really do not believe are important ...

What I do that is not   Why I do this   Why it is not important
important to me

5.   I have been confused or uncertain about my personal values in these circumstances ...

My dilemmas   Reasons for confusion/   What I actually did
                            uncertainty

6.   The primary influences that have shaped my key values are ...

Influences which shaped my   How my values were influenced
values

Reproduced from *Developing Your People: Easy-to-use activities for improving management skills*
by Mike Woodcock and Dave Francis, Gower, Aldershot

7. These are the values that other people hold but that I find unacceptable or unattractive ...

    Values held by others   Reasons for being
                                    unacceptable/unattractive

8. Looking back over the past ten years, I wish I had pursued these values more ...

    Wanted values   Reasons not pursued

9. In my job I strive to ...

    Emphasize these things   Discourage these things

10. I believe that other people would say the following about me:

a)

b)

c)

Reproduced from *Developing Your People: Easy-to-use activities for improving management skills*
by Mike Woodcock and Dave Francis, Gower, Aldershot

Clarifying values*

Clarifying values should be undertaken systematically. Much of the information comes from within your experiences, beliefs, and feelings. Values clarification is one of the few topics where inner beliefs are more important than external analysis.

Clarified values meet the following eight conditions:

1. *Values must be chosen from alternatives.* Only values that have been positively chosen will be firmly held. The act of choosing strengthens commitment. You must debate issues of principle in order to choose those values for which you are prepared to fight. For such debates to be meaningful, people need to consider the issues raised in the Values questionnaire.

2. *Values must be consistent with each other.* Values must support each other. Values pulling in different directions are destructive. Each of us must study the package of values that he or she lives by and check that they are intellectually and behaviourally consistent.

3. *Values must be limited in number.* An excessive number of values dissipates effort and is confusing. Values are broad, deep, and general. It would be foolish to have dozens of values, as these undermine clarity. It is far better to search for those things that you find really important.

4. *Values must be actionable.* A value that cannot be put into effect becomes a weakness; an individual should not be committed to an impossibility. You should take great care not to incorporate pious hopes into your own value statements. All values should be submitted to the 'for instance test'. Cases must be tested against the espoused value to see whether it holds up in all situations.

5. *Values must enhance performance.* Values are an enabling device; they are a means of shaping behaviour. Values clarification is part of the development of a personal effectiveness strategy. There must be a logical relationship between the personal key success factors and the values adopted.

6. *Values must be attractive and instil pride.* People should be uplifted by their values. They should feel proud of their beliefs. Values must be capable of being respected. Only when values are attractive to the individual will energy be invested in making them a reality.

7. *Values must be capable of being communicated.* Only when a value can be

---

* Taken from Mike Woodcock and Dave Francis, *Clarifying Organizational Values*, Aldershot: Gower, 1989.

communicated is it clear enough to hold. You should not adopt a value unless it is capable of being demonstrated. When you are willing to stand up and admit your beliefs, your values have been clarified.

8. *Values must be written.* Until a set of values is clear enough to be committed to paper, it will not have the authority to be a personal statement. The act of writing down values has three benefits: it clarifies the mind, provokes debate, and provides a message that can be communicated. When the attempt is made to write values down, any logical flaws will appear.

Values clarification exercise

Directions

With one or two other people, discuss the results of the Values questionnaire. Choose others with whom you feel comfortable. Only disclose what you wish. Keep the conversation in strict confidence. Consider each individual in turn, with the others acting as counsellors. Answer the items below for each person separately. Allow approximately equal time for each individual.

1. In completing the Values questionnaire ...

I was surprised by:

I was pleased by:

I found difficult:

I was concerned by:

I found these contradictions:

I was unclear about:

I learned:

2. These are the values that I prize:

a)

b)

c)

d)

e)

3. This cartoon represents my personal values.

4. These are the issues that I need to explore further:

Issues to explore   Why?   How?

CLARIFYING PERSONAL VALUES

1 VALUES MUST BE CHOSEN FROM ALTERNATIVES

2 VALUES MUST BE CONSISTENT WITH EACH OTHER

3 VALUES MUST BE LIMITED IN NUMBER

4 VALUES MUST BE ACTIONABLE

5 VALUES MUST ENHANCE PERFORMANCE

6 VALUES MUST BE ATTRACTIVE AND INSTIL PRIDE

7 VALUES MUST BE CAPABLE OF BEING COMMUNICATED

8 VALUES MUST BE WRITTEN

5

Managerial values questionnaire

Objectives

- To explore values related to managerial success.
- To contribute to values clarification for managers.

Group size

Any number.

Time required

1 hour 30 minutes.

Materials required

1. Task sheet 5.1: Managerial values questionnaire.
2. Task sheet 5.2: Managerial values questionnaire: scoring and explanation.
3. Task sheet 5.3: Exercise.
4. OHP 5.1.

Description

To provide a definition of values associated with success and to ask participants to evaluate the extent to which their values are helping them to succeed.

	Method	Approx time
1	Introduce the activity and ask each participant to complete Task sheet 5.1: Managerial values questionnaire.	15 mins
2	Give a brief presentation on the 12 values for managerial success using OHP 5.1: The Woodcock–Francis values wheel. Explain that the values model presented gives one interpretation of success and other models are possible. However, for the purpose of the exercise, participants are asked to accept the model as given.	10 mins
3	Instruct participants to score their questionnaire using Task sheet 5.2 and invite them to read the brief explanation of the 12 value areas.	10 mins
4	Form small groups (pairs or trios) and ask them to work through Task sheet 5.3: Exercise, as directed.	45 mins
5	Gather all participants together and ask each individual to share an insight gained through participation in the exercise.	10 mins

Managerial values questionnaire

Answer the 60 items below about yourself. Please give your opinion on each item. Allocate points as shown:

The statement is:

Totally true	4 points
Largely true	3 points
Neither true nor false	2 points
Largely untrue	1 point
Totally untrue	0 points

The 60 items:

1. I act in ways which demonstrate that I am 'in charge'.   (Score_____)

2. I invest considerable effort in developing others.   (Score_____)

3. I recognize outstanding performance.   (Score_____)

4. I take great care to ensure that key decisions are well considered.   (Score_____)

5. I constantly search for ways to do things more efficiently. (Score_____)

6. I avoid spending money unnecessarily.   (Score_____)

7. I treat people with genuine difficulties with compassion. (Score_____)

8. I take care to ensure that everyone feels part of a team.   (Score_____)

9. I work hard to be fair.   (Score_____)

10. I am aggressive in defence of my own interests.   (Score_____)

11. I ensure that everyone is aware of the importance of care for the customer.   (Score_____)

12. I encourage innovation and creativity.   (Score_____)

13. I accept responsibility.   (Score_____)

14. I recruit staff with great care.   (Score_____)

15. I ensure that my staff receive regular feedback on how they are performing.   (Score_____)

16. I take critical decisions only after very careful analysis.   (Score_____)

17. I investigate new technologies and techniques to see whether they could increase efficiency.   (Score_____)

Reproduced from *Developing Your People: Easy-to-use activities for improving management skills*
by Mike Woodcock and Dave Francis, Gower, Aldershot

18. I make great efforts to ensure that people understand the economic contribution they are making. (Score_____)

19. I always give a fair hearing to all parties when disputes arise. (Score_____)

20. I deliberately build teams. (Score_____)

21. I abide by a strict code of conduct. (Score_____)

22. I am watchful to reduce threats to my organization. (Score_____)

23. I believe that my organization must be 'competitive with the best'. (Score_____)

24. I value new ideas. (Score_____)

25. I am willing to exercise authority. (Score_____)

26. I make great efforts to develop the skills of others. (Score_____)

27. I link managerial rewards to performance. (Score_____)

28. I plan with care. (Score_____)

29. My part of the organization is dedicated to high quality. (Score_____)

30. I ensure my unit is cost-effective. (Score_____)

31. I demonstrate by my actions that I care about the well-being of the people in the organization. (Score_____)

32. I create a positive atmosphere so that employees strongly identify with their work unit. (Score_____)

33. I ensure that codes of conduct are well understood. (Score_____)

34. I build support for my unit from those who can provide resources. (Score_____)

35. In encourage competition between work groups to raise standards of performance. (Score_____)

36. I am ready to seize opportunities as they occur. (Score_____)

37. I support those with responsibilities by giving them commensurate authority. (Score_____)

38. I help others to develop their careers. (Score_____)

39. Performance is the main criterion by which I evaluate others. (Score_____)

40. I communicate decisions effectively. (Score_____)

41. I will not tolerate low standards. (Score_____)

42. I systematically compare my unit against others. (Score_____)

Reproduced from *Developing Your People: Easy-to-use activities for improving management skills*
by Mike Woodcock and Dave Francis, Gower, Aldershot

43. I am considered by others to be a 'good boss'. (Score_____)

44. I encourage people to go out of their way to be helpful to each other. (Score_____)

45. I ensure that internal rules and regulations are fair. (Score_____)

46. I am active in dealing with anything or anyone that could inhibit success. (Score_____)

47. I take steps to avoid destructive competition between departments. (Score_____)

48. I encourage entrepreneurial skills. (Score_____)

49. I keep my organization 'on course'. (Score_____)

50. I regularly evaluate the performance of everyone who works for me. (Score_____)

51. I reward people for doing things that enable the organization to be successful. (Score_____)

52. I insist that people use systematic decision-making techniques. (Score_____)

53. I build 'pride in the job'. (Score_____)

54. I use financial resources prudently. (Score_____)

55. There are no destructive class or racial barriers in my part of the organization. (Score_____)

56. I take deliberate steps to develop effective teamwork. (Score_____)

57. I ensure that rules help, rather than hinder, work accomplishment. (Score_____)

58. I fight to protect the organization's interests. (Score_____)

59. I ensure that competitiveness in relation to other companies is regularly measured. (Score_____)

60. I support good ideas. (Score_____)

Managerial values questionnaire: scoring and explanation

Answer sheet

Write your score against each item number, then total the horizontal columns.

TOTALS

1	13	25	37	49		Power: 'I manage'
2	14	26	38	50		Performance: 'I support the best'
3	15	27	39	51		Reward: 'I ensure that performance determines benefts'
4	16	28	40	52		Effectiveness: 'I do the right things'
5	17	29	41	53		Efficiency: 'I do things right'
6	18	30	42	54		Economy: 'I am economical'
7	19	31	43	55		Fairness: 'I care'
8	20	32	44	56		Teamwork: 'I build teams'
9	21	33	45	57		Law and order: 'I am just'
10	22	34	46	58		Defence: 'I know my enemy'
11	23	35	47	59		Competitiveness: 'I am strong'
12	24	36	48	60		Opportunism: 'I dare'

Interpreting the questionnaire

You have now scored the questionnaire and are no doubt wondering what it means.

You have a score for each of the 12 managerial values identified on the right-hand side of the answer sheet. High scores indicate a strong value, low scores suggest a weakness!

Read the brief descriptions of successful managerial values that follow and then complete the exercise as directed.

The 12 managerial values

I POWER

You have the knowledge, authority, and position to acquire resources and make decisions. The successful manager understands the inherent power of his/her position and takes charge. This value is practised as: 'I manage'.

II PERFORMANCE

The management task is complex and important. The quality of people who fill roles is significant. An inadequate manager can wreak havoc – both by sins of commission and by sins of omission. The successful manager understands the vital importance of employing the best possible candidates for jobs and of continuously developing their competency. This value is practised as: 'I support the best'.

III REWARD

As performance is important, all employees need to perform consistently and energetically in pursuit of the organization's goals. The successful manager identifies and rewards success. This value is practised as: 'I ensure performance determines benefit'.

IV EFFECTIVENESS

Identifying the right issues must be a constant concern. A successful manager is able to concentrate resources on activities that get results. This value is practised as: 'I do the right things'.

V EFFICIENCY

It has been said that good management consists of doing hundreds of little things well. All too often a small error has a disproportionate effect on the

87

quality of the whole. The drive to do everything well gives a sharp edge. The successful manager relentlessly searches for better ways to do things, and constantly builds pride into the job. This value is practised as: 'I do things right'.

VI ECONOMY

It is a great deal easier to spend money than to earn it. Lack of effective cost control is a common cause of business failure and organizational waste. The discipline rendered by the profit and loss account endows the wise manager with the ultimate measure of success. Every activity costs money; someone, somewhere, has to pay. The successful manager understands the importance of facing economic reality. This value is practised as: 'I am economical'.

VII FAIRNESS

One of the greatest compliments paid to a good teacher is that he or she is 'firm but fair'. Managers, by their actions, greatly affect people's lives, both in work and outside. What they do, and what they refuse to do, has a significant impact on the quality of life of all employees. Using this power with compassion and fairness builds trust and commitment. The successful manager realizes that people's views, perceptions, and feelings are important. This value is practised as: 'I care'.

VIII TEAMWORK

A well-organized and well-motivated group can achieve more than the sum of the individuals who comprise the group. People enjoy the company of others and can work well collectively. One person's talents can balance the weaknesses of another. It is vitally important that people feel that they belong. The successful manager ensures that s/he derives the benefits of effective teamwork. This value is practised as: 'I build teams'.

IX LAW AND ORDER

Every community develops a framework of laws that regulate conduct. These provide the ground rules of acceptable behaviour. A manager exercises considerable power over the lives of others, sometimes operating as judge and jury, often without a right of appeal. The successful manager devises and honourably administers an appropriate system of rules and regulations. This value is practised as: 'I am just'.

X DEFENCE

For many organizations it is a dog-eat-dog world. In every commercial organization, there are talented people planning strategies to increase their business at the expense of the competition. Many noncommercial organizations find themselves under threat from those who provide their funds. The successful manager studies external threats and then formulates a strong defence. This value is practised as: 'I know my enemy'.

XI   COMPETITIVENESS

The capacity to be competitive is the only sure-fire recipe for survival. The successful manager takes all necessary steps to be competitive. It is the best who survive and the weakest who go to the wall. This value is practised as: 'I am strong'.

XII   OPPORTUNISM

Despite the most brilliant planning, it is inevitable that unexpected opportunities and threats will occur. A manager cannot afford to ignore the unexpected. It is wiser actively to seek out new opportunities than to allow others, more fleet of foot, to grab the best chances. Opportunities have to be seized quickly, even though this may involve risks. The successful manager is a committed opportunist. This value is practised as: 'I dare'.

Exercise

In discussion with at least one other person, complete the following:

1. These are my strongest managerial values:

STRONGEST VALUES	HOW I BEHAVE TO IMPLEMENT THESE
a	
b	
c	

2. These are my least strong managerial values:

WEAKEST VALUES	EFFECTS
a	
b	
c	

90

3. Strengthening these values would be positive for me.

I WOULD LIKE TO STRENGTHEN THESE VALUES	BENEFITS	DISADVANTAGES	I WOULD NEED TO BEHAVE DIFFERENTLY IN THESE WAYS

The Woodcock–Francis values wheel

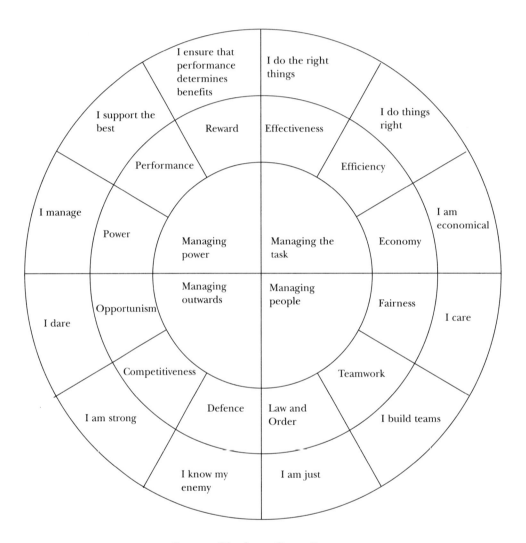

Inner Circle = Core Issues
Middle Circle = Sub-issues Arising from Core Issues
Outer Circle = Values

6

Cave rescue*

Objectives

- To enable managers to study the impact of values on decision making.
- To develop skill in information analysis.
- To enable managers to practise consensus-seeking behaviour.

Group size

This is a group activity for four to eight persons. Participation should be voluntary.

Time required

1 hour 25 minutes.

Materials required

1. Handout 6.1: Cave rescue briefing sheet.
2. Handout 6.2: Volunteers' personal details sheet.

* © Challenge Ltd. Adapted from the 'Cave Rescue' activity in M. Woodcock, *Team Development Manual* (Aldershot: Gower, 1979) and in D. Francis and D. Young, *Improving Work Groups. A Practical Manual for Team Building* (San Diego, CA: University Associates, 1979).

3. Task sheet 6.1: Ranking sheet.

4. Task sheet 6.2: Review sheet.

Description

This activity is helpful in clarifying personal values, improving problem-solving skills, increasing influence and developing team-building skills.

Method		Approx time
1	Distribute a copy of Handout 6.1: Cave rescue briefing sheet, 6.2: Volunteers' personal details sheet and Task sheet 6.1: Ranking sheet, to each participant. During the activity, the facilitator will keep time.	50 mins
2	At the end of the task, distribute a copy of Task sheet 6.2: Review sheet, to each participant, and ask them to complete it.	5 mins
3	Lead a review discussion and conclude the session by asking, 'What learning from this activity may be useful in our daily work?'	30 mins

Cave rescue briefing sheet

Your group is asked to take the role of a research management committee who are funding projects into human behaviour in confined spaces.

You have been called to an emergency meeting as one of the experiments has gone badly wrong.

Six volunteers have been taken into a cave system in a remote part of the country, connected only by a radio link to the research hut by the cave entrance. It was intended that the volunteers would spend four days underground but they have been trapped by falling rocks and rising water.

The only rescue team available tells you that rescue will be extremely difficult and only one person can be brought out each hour with the equipment at their disposal. It is likely that the rapidly rising water will drown some of the volunteers before rescue can be effected.

The volunteers are aware of the dangers of their plight. They have contacted the research hut using the radio link and said that they are unwilling to take a decision as to the sequence by which they will be rescued. By the terms of the Research Project, the responsibility for making this decision now rests with your committee.

Life-saving equipment will arrive in 50 minutes at the cave entrance and you will need to advise the team of the order for rescue by completing the ranking sheet.

The only information you have available is drawn from the project files and is reproduced on the volunteers' personal details sheet. You may use any criteria you think fit to help you make a decision.

Volunteers' personal details sheet

Volunteer 1:   Helen

Helen is 34 years old and is a housewife. She has four children aged between 7 months and 8 years. Her hobbies are ice skating and cooking. She lives in a pleasant house in Gloucester, and was born in England. Helen is known to have developed a covert romantic and sexual relationship with another volunteer (Owen).

Volunteer 2:   Tozo

Tozo is 19 years old and a sociology student at Keele University. She is the daughter of wealthy Japanese parents who live in Tokyo. Her father is an industrialist who is also a national authority on traditional Japanese mime theatre. Tozo is unmarried but has several high-born suitors as she is outstandingly attractive. She has recently been the subject of a TV documentary on Japanese womanhood and flower arranging.

Volunteer 3:   Jobe

Jobe is a man of 41 years and was born in Central Africa. He is a minister of religion whose life work has been devoted to the social and political evolution of African peoples. Jobe is a founder member of RAGRAT – the Radical Action Group for the Reoccupation of All Towns. RAGRAT has been described as 'an urban terrorist movement more dangerous than the Animal Liberation Front'. He has made several study visits to the People's Republic of China. He is married with eleven children whose ages range from 6 years to 19 years. His hobby is playing in a jazz band.

Volunteer 4:   Owen

Owen is an unmarried man of 27 years. As a short-commission officer he spent part of his service in Northern Ireland where, as an undercover agent, he broke up an IRA cell and received a special commendation in despatches. Since returning to civilian life he has been unsettled and drinking has become a persistent problem. At present he is a Youth Adventure Leader, devoting much energy to helping young people and leading caving groups. His recreation is preparing and driving stock cars. He lives in Brecon, South Wales.

Reproduced from *Developing Your People: Easy-to-use activities for improving management skills* by Mike Woodcock and Dave Francis, Gower, Aldershot

Volunteer 5: Paul

Paul is a man of 42 who has been divorced for six years. His ex-wife is now happily re-married. He was born in Scotland, but now lives in Richmond, Surrey. Paul works as a medical research scientist at the Hammersmith Hospital and he is recognized as a world authority on the treatment of rabies. He has recently developed a low-cost treatment which could be self-administered. Much of the research data is still in his working notebooks. Unfortunately, Paul has experienced some emotional difficulties in recent years and has twice been convicted of indecent exposure. The last occasion was 11 months ago. His hobbies are classical music, opera and sailing.

Volunteer 6: Edward

Edward is a man of 59 years who has lived and worked in Barnsley for most of his life. He is general manager of a factory producing rubber belts for machines. The factory employs 71 persons. he is prominent in local society, and is a Freemason and a Conservative councillor. He is married with two children who have their own families and have moved away from Barnsley. Edward has recently returned from Poland where he was personally responsible for promoting a contract to supply large numbers of industrial belts over a five-year period. This contract, if signed, would mean work for another 25 people. Edward's hobbies include collecting antique guns and he intends to write a book about Civil War Armaments on his retirement. He is also a strong cricket supporter.

Reproduced from *Developing Your People: Easy-to-use activities for improving management skills*
by Mike Woodcock and Dave Francis, Gower, Aldershot

Ranking sheet

Your group is to rank the six trapped individuals. Write each of the volunteers' names next to the number that indicates the order of rescue.

Order of Rescue	Name
1.	
2.	
3.	
4.	
5.	
6.	

Review sheet

1. What were the principal criteria used in ranking the volunteers?

2. How closely did the group's criteria line up with your own?

3. How comfortable did you feel about making this kind of decision?

4. What behaviours helped the group in arriving at a decision?

5. What behaviours hindered the group in arriving at a decision?

7

Boot Camp

Objectives

- To provide an opportunity for a group to explore the interrelationship between values and decision making.

- To explore decision making where individuals operate from different value systems.

- To develop skills in group decision making.

Group size

Any number of participants can undertake this activity at the same time but there is a minimum group size (four people).

Time required

1 hour 10 minutes.

Materials required

1. Handout 7.1: Boot Camp briefing sheet.

2. Task sheet 7.1: Boot Camp training plan.

3. Handout 7.2: Boot Camp analysis, and the UK Home Office Boot Camp Training Plan 1995.

4. Task sheet 7.2: Boot Camp review.

5. OHP 7.1.

Description

To provide a case example that will enable participants to clarify their own values on a contentious issue and see the effect that an individual's values have on management policies.

Method		Approx time
1	Introduce the activity by discussing Handout 7.1: Boot Camp briefing sheet and Task sheet 7.1: Boot Camp training plan. Use OHP 7.1: Values in groups, to brief participants.	10 mins
2	Ask participants to complete Task sheet 7.1: Boot Camp training plan.	30 mins
3	Give out Handout 7.2: Boot Camp analysis.	5 mins
4	Distribute Task sheet 7.2: Boot Camp review and ask participants to complete it.	25 mins

Boot Camp briefing sheet

In many countries of the world there are great difficulties in dealing with young offenders. Prison is seen as a 'university of crime' and young people's detention centres contain but do not seem successful in reforming. There is a continual search for more effective ways of treating young offenders.

In the early 1990s the 'Boot Camp' approach was developed in the USA. The aim was to punish, deter and reform young criminals. A strict military-style discipline was supplemented by education.

Your task

You are asked to assume that your group has been appointed by the government agency responsible for prisons to act as lay advisers on the design of the Boot Camp regime to be a new pilot scheme which will be introduced next year.

You are asked to complete the Boot Camp Training Plan on the next page based on your group's beliefs about what regime will have the greatest likelihood of being successful. You may base your Training Plan recommendation on existing schemes but it is your views that are required. You should reach decisions by consensus.

Boot Camp training plan

Questions	Group answers
What key objectives will the Boot Camp strive for?	1. 2. 3.
What activities will fill the day? Account for each waking hour.	0500 0530 0600 0630 0700 0730 0800 0830 0900 0930 1000 1030 1100 1130 1200 1230 1300 1330 1400 1430 1500

Questions	Group answers
	1530
	1600
	1630
	1700
	1730
	1800
	1830
	1900
	1930
	2000
	2030
	2100
	2200
	2230
	2300
What will be the approach to reward and punishment?	
How long should offenders stay?	

Boot Camp analysis

The task you have just undertaken repeats an exercise conducted by the UK Home Office in 1995. You are asked to look at the Home Office's answers to the Training plan questions and then review the exercise as suggested (Task sheet 7.2).

UK Home Office Boot Camp Training Plan 1995

Questions	Group answers
What key objectives will the Boot Camp strive for?	1. Self-respect. 2. Respect for authority and society. 3. Self-development.
What activities will fill the day?	0600 Wake. Make bed. Clean. Have snack. 0630 Full kit inspection on parade ground. 0710 Lukewarm shower. 0730 Room and communal area inspection to ensure 'immaculate' standards. 0800 Breakfast. 0830 Anger Management Training (programmes on crime, drugs etc.). 0945 Basic education (numeracy and literacy). 1100 Coping skills (personal hygiene and budget management). 1215 Lunch. 1245 Quiet period for writing up log book on morning's work. 1315 Physical Education (running, circuit training and assault course). 1415 Shower. 1430 Skills training (vocational skills). 1700 Dinner. 1730 Quiet period, log book entries.

Reproduced from *Developing Your People: Easy-to-use activities for improving management skills*
by Mike Woodcock and Dave Francis, Gower, Aldershot

Questions	Group answers
	1800 Social responsibility session (to include visits by victims of crime to make offenders aware of the effects of their behaviour).
	1900 Helping the disadvantaged (e.g. handicrafts for charity and helping the disabled).
	2000 Group meeting (assessment of day; peer pressure on those 'not pulling their weight').
	2100 Hot drink. Those with credit points can watch television etc.
	2145 Wash.
	2200 Lights out, no talking.
What will be the approach to reward and punishment?	The regime will be very strict. Behaviour will be closely supervised. Only those who conform in detail to the rules will earn 'credits' – to be spent listening to the radio, watching TV etc.
How long should offenders stay?	6 months.

Boot Camp review

Answer the following questions as a group.

Questions	Group answers
1. What are the similarities between the recommendations of your group and those of the Home Office?	
2. What are the differences between the recommendations of your group and the Home Office?	
3. What beliefs and values underpin your Training plan? (i.e. what were your assumptions about 'good' reforming institutions for young offenders?)	
4. What methods did you use to develop an understanding of each group member's viewpoint?	
5. Reflect on any significant differences of view between group members. How were these resolved?	

Reproduced from *Developing Your People: Easy-to-use activities for improving management skills* by Mike Woodcock and Dave Francis, Gower, Aldershot

Questions	Group answers	
6. To what extent were your group's values agreed and explicit before you began to develop the regime?		
7. How effective were you in finding activities which would put your values into action?		
8. If you were to tackle a similar exercise again what would you do in the same way and what would you change?	Behaviours to be repeated	Behaviours not to be repeated

Reproduced from *Developing Your People: Easy-to-use activities for improving management skills* by Mike Woodcock and Dave Francis, Gower, Aldershot

VALUES IN GROUPS

MAKE STEP-BY-STEP PROGRESS

→ CLARIFY ALL THE VALUE ISSUES

→ ASK EACH INDIVIDUAL TO EXPLAIN HIS/HER VALUE POSITIONS

→ QUESTIONS FOR CLARIFICATION ONLY

→ IDENTIFY COMMON GROUND

→ IDENTIFY DIFFERENCES

→ TAKE EACH DIFFERENCE AND DEBATE – EXAMINE THE IMPLICATIONS OF EACH OPTION

→ AGREE YOUR GROUP POSITION (INDIVIDUALS MUST BE PREPARED TO GIVE SUPPORT EVEN IF THEY DON'T AGREE)

Reproduced from *Developing Your People: Easy-to-use activities for improving management skills* by Mike Woodcock and Dave Francis, Gower, Aldershot

8

Manager's audit of communication effectiveness (MACE)*

Objectives

- To clarify communication competencies for managers.
- To assist managers in planning how to improve their personal communication skills.

Group size

1. MACE is best conducted in pairs or trios, although it can also be completed by a manager working alone.

2. As many pairs or trios as desired can work at the same time.

3. Quiet places for discussion are required.

Time required

1 hour 25 minutes.

Materials required

1. Task sheet 8.1: The MACE questionnaire.

2. Task sheet 8.2: MACE answer grid.

* This is an amended version of an activity first published in *50 Activities for Unblocking Organizational Communication* Volume 2, by Dave Francis (Gower, 1991).

3. Task sheet 8.3: MACE questionnaire interpretation.

4. Handout 8.1: The 12 components of communication effectiveness.

5. Task sheet 8.4: MACE action planning sheet.

6. OHP 8.1.

7. Flipchart.

8. Quiet places for discussion.

Description

This activity enables managers to review their personal effectiveness as communicators. It was designed for management training programmes but can be adapted for use in management education, counselling and team-building programmes.

MACE is based on the model used in *Unblocking Organizational Communication* by Dave Francis (Gower, 1987). It is helpful to study the underlying concepts before using the questionnaire.

	Method	Approx time
1	Introduce the activity and summarize the objectives.	5 mins
2	Give each participant a copy of Task sheet 8.1: The MACE questionnaire and ask them to complete the inventory.	20 mins
3	Distribute Task sheet 8.2: MACE answer grid, Task sheet 8.3: MACE questionnaire interpretation, Handout 8.1: The 12 components of communication effectiveness, and Task sheet 8.4: MACE action planning sheet. A short presentation (using OHP 8.1) summarizing the theory can be given at this stage. Ask participants to complete the answer grid.	15 mins
4	Ask participants to discuss their results with one or two others before completing Task sheet 8.4: MACE action planning sheet. They should assist each other by asking questions, suggesting ideas and clarifying thinking.	30 mins
5	Gather the group together and review communication skills. Note key points on a flipchart.	15 mins

The MACE questionnaire

This questionnaire examines how you, as an individual, communicate within your organization. Consider each of the 36 statements below and circle the most appropriate answer. Be as objective and honest as you can.

1. In the last 6 months I have been in contact with people outside my organization who have helped me keep up to date in my job.

many people	3 points
few people	2 points
one person	1 point
no one	0 points

2. I have clear ideas about how the work of my department will change in the future.

true	3 points
partly true	1 point
untrue	0 points

3. I succeed whenever I need to persuade someone to my point of view.

always true	3 points
usually true	2 points
sometimes true	1 point
untrue	0 points

4. In the past 6 months I have organized meetings with others at my level to improve co-ordination.

many meetings	3 points
a few meetings	2 points
one meeting	1 point
no meetings	0 points

5. I have taken every possible step to ensure that my people have good facilities for meetings.

true	3 points
partly true	1 point
untrue	0 points

6. I give detailed feedback to my subordinates on their performance.

monthly (or more often)	3 points
between monthly and quarterly	2 points
between quarterly and annually	1point
never	0 points

113

Reproduced from *Developing Your People: Easy-to-use activities for improving management skills*
by Mike Woodcock and Dave Francis, Gower, Aldershot

7. I could never be justly accused of saying one thing and doing another.

true	3 points
largely true	1 point
untrue	0 points

8. When I recruit a new person I am unconcerned as to whether a man or woman gets the job.

true	3 points
untrue	0 points

9. Other people have told me that the meetings I run are productive.

many people	3 points
few people	2 points
one person	1 point
no one	0 points

10. I go out of my way to find out how people feel about what is going on in the organization.

true	3 points
partly true	1 point
untrue	0 points

11. In my team or department I have cut unnecessary red tape to the minimum.

true	3 points
partly true	1 point
untrue	0 points

12. I have been thoroughly trained in both written and oral communication.

more than 5 days' training	3 points
between 1 and 5 days' training	1 point
one day's training or less	0 points

13. I spend time keeping up to date with developments in my specialism.

more than 4 hours each week	3 points
between 1 and 4 hours per week	2 points
less than 1 hour per week	1 point
no time	0 points

14. Other people have told me that my formal presentations about future plans are well thought out.

many people	3 points
few people	2 points
one person	1 point
no one	0 points

15. People have told me that I am very effective at exerting influence on others.

many people	3 points
few people	2 points
one person	1 point
no one	0 points

16. I develop systems to link the work of my unit or department with others with whom we are interdependent.

true	3 points
partly true	1 point
untrue	0 points

17. When 'geography' prevents easy communication I take action to reduce the difficulties to an absolute minimum.

effective action	3 points
partly effective action	2 points
no action	0 points

18. Today, any of my subordinates will be able to say how their job performance is being measured.

true	3 points
partly true	1 point
untrue	0 points

19. I have taken action to encourage an atmosphere of trust and openness in my part of the organization.

many actions	3 points
some actions	2 points
1 or 2 actions	1 point
no action	0 points

20. I take effective action whenever I detect that someone in my organization is the target of prejudice.

true	3 points
partly true	1 point
untrue	0 points

21. I have built the people who report to me into a close and effective team.

true	3 points
partly true	1 point
untrue	0 points

115

22. People have told me that I am very 'approachable'.

many people	3 points
a few people	2 points
one person	1 point
no one	0 points

23. I have carefully studied how information technology developments can enhance the work of my department/organization.

true	3 points
partly true	1 point
untrue	0 points

24. In the last 6 months I have been told that I am 'a good listener'.

many people	3 points
a few people	2 points
one person	1 point
no one	0 points

25. I spend time finding out what factors in the external environment might affect my operation in the future.

more than 3 hours weekly	3 points
1–3 hours weekly	2 points
less than 1 hour weekly	1 point
no time	0 points

26. Today, everyone in my team would agree that our performance is vital to the success of the organization.

true	3 points
largely true	2 points
partly true	1 point
untrue	0 points

27. I work hard to convince my staff that senior management's plans are well conceived.

true	3 points
partly true	1 point
untrue	0 points

28. By my personal example I encourage people to relate with other departments to break down barriers.

true	3 points
partly true	1 point
untrue	0 points

29. After discussions with people in my part of the organization we have made it easy for people to communicate informally with each other.

true	3 points
partly true	1 point
untrue	0 points

30. All my subordinates receive formal regular briefing on what is going on in the organization.

at least fortnightly	3 points
at least monthly	1 point
almost never	0 points

31. I spend time 'walking about' and letting my people get to know me.

more than 7 hours weekly	3 points
2–7 hours weekly	2 points
30 minutes to 2 hours weekly	1 point
no time	0 points

32. Should differences of colour, creed, social class or age influence relationships in my part of the organization, I take immediate action to reduce the problem.

always	3 points
sometimes	1 point
never	0 points

33. I develop teams which are effective at solving problems.

true	3 points
partly true	1 point
untrue	0 points

34. I have an effective formal system which enables accurate information to flow upwards so that I can take valid decisions.

true	3 points
partly true	1 point
untrue	0 points

35. I cut out all unnecessary paperwork.

true	3 points
largely true	2 points
untrue	0 points

36. Others have commented favourably upon the quality of my oral and written reports.

many people	3 points
a few people	2 points
one person	1 point
no one	0 points

MACE answer grid

Copy your scores from the questionnaire on to the grid below. Add the totals horizontally and place the score in the box provided.

Totals

1		13		25		I
2		14		26		II
3		15		27		III
4		16		28		IV
5		17		29		V
6		18		30		VI
7		19		31		VII
8		20		32		VIII
9		21		33		IX
10		22		34		X
11		23		35		XI
12		24		36		XII

MACE questionnaire: interpretation

You have now completed the Manager's Audit of Communication Effectiveness. Check that you have added the three scores on each horizontal line and written the totals in the final column. Do this for each of the 12 lines. These are your scores for each component of communication effectiveness. A high score indicates a strength, a lower score suggests a weaker area. Remember that this is a self-assessment, so your results may not be objectively valid. The purpose is to start you thinking about your own communication skills from an analytical viewpoint.

Copy the totals from the answer grid onto the table below.

	YOUR TOTALS	COMMUNICATION COMPONENT
I		Being sensitive to the external environment
II		Having a compelling vision
III		Being persuasive
IV		Constructing integrating mechanisms
V		Managing the physical environment
VI		Maintaining downwards flow
VII		Generating trust
VIII		Combating prejudice
IX		Developing teams
X		Maintaining upwards flow
XI		Fighting red tape
XII		Demonstrating communication skills

You now have an indication of your strength in each of the 12 components of communication. However, the headlines used to define the components mean little in themselves. Review the longer definitions for each component given in Handout 8.1: The 12 components of communication effectiveness to understand more clearly what each means. Pay particular attention to any low-scoring components.

119

The 12 components of communication effectiveness

Component I: Being sensitive to the external environment

If you have a high score on this component you are alert, closely in touch with the world outside. You communicate with the environment. You identify opportunities and threats. Information from the environment is used to track what is going on. You are an 'open system' which constantly adapts to changing circumstances. You adopt the view that everyone should keep their eyes and ears open. You study the environment so that you can continue to be competitive in tomorrow's world. You keep up to date with new techniques, ideas and developments.

Component II: Having a compelling vision

If you have a high score on this component you are focused, heading for clear goals. You communicate the identity of your part of the organization and define where it is heading. This is expressed as a 'vision of the future' that is seen to be important, coherent and sustainable. Inspiration, excitement, farsightedness, great clarity, and good judgement are qualities that you possess. Your 'vision' is the primary energizing force in your part of the organization. It may be expressed in words but, most importantly, the vision should be shared by all your team members.

Component III: Being persuasive

If you have a high score on this component you attract others, encouraging people to follow. You have the communication strategies and skills to encourage people to play a part in transforming the 'vision' into reality. You form attitudes, change behaviour, instil standards and build a positive climate. You are able to 'sell' the importance of working together for a common cause. You recognize that persuasion techniques are useless unless they are reinforced by behaviour. What people do communicates more persuasively than what they say.

Component IV: Constructing integrating mechanisms

If you have a high score on this component you co-ordinate organizations, ensuring that there are adequate mechanisms to integrate effort. You realize that organizations all develop specialists, departments and groups. All these must be integrated, so that they work together for the benefit of the organization as a whole. You devise communication mechanisms to enable necessary integration to take place. You understand that the needs for integration vary with the size of the organization and the types of work undertaken. You adapt your methods to routine, professional, divisionalized and creative organizations. You recognize that organizations which lack well-developed integrating mechanisms are inefficient, wasteful, incompetent, ponderous, uncreative and fragmented.

Component V: Managing the physical environment

If you have a high score on this component you are concerned that the lay-out of the organization encourages necessary communication. You realize that local geography greatly influences communication patterns and, unfortunately, many architects and planners have paid scant attention to the human consequences of their designs. The result is disintegration of both formal and informal communication. You assess individual work patterns and help by improving the lay-out of their workplace. You understand that teams should be physically close and relate easily with other teams across boundaries. You make intelligent use of electronic media to reduce communication blockages caused by geographical inconvenience.

Component VI: Maintaining downwards flow

If you have a high score on this component you are directive, ensuring that people are told what they should know to play their part. You realize that only those with seniority can see the 'whole picture'. Objectives, policies, procedures, disciplines, success measures, controls and directives all need to be reliably cascaded down. This is a necessary integrating force. You control as appropriate: by action planning, performance control or the enforcement of company policies. You cause the flow of information downwards by one of these four methods: down the line, through representatives of the workforce, by methods of mass communication or using techniques of training and indoctrination.

Component VII: Generating trust

If you have a high score on this component you are honourable: people trust you. People know that they can rely on you. You understand that, when there is insufficient trust, communication suffers badly; what is said is not believed. You help to sustain a healthy community by stimulating constructive relationships and encouraging goodwill. You know that self-interest, if carried to extremes, is destructive to organizations and that trust cannot be

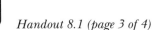

manufactured by deception; you will only be trusted if you behave in trustworthy ways. You are honest, consistent, realistic, follow through and act fairly and decently. You behave with integrity and principle, understanding that, once destroyed, trust can only be rebuilt with painful slowness.

Component VIII: Combating prejudice

If you have a high score on this component you are fair, making sure that no category of people is disadvantaged. You do not treat any group as inferior. Such prejudiced attitudes cause serious communication problems. You feel deeply that healthy communities are based on the principle of fairness. You do not express prejudice in word or deed – whether racial, sexual, religious or between social classes. You know that prejudice is destructive because it increases social distance and decreases humanness. You realize that this is particularly damaging because prejudice is often energized by aggression and hostility. Then energy is absorbed by conflict, and unfairness undermines a sense of unity.

Component IX: Developing teams

If you have a high score on this component you encourage co-operation, helping people to work well together. You realize that teamwork, in all its forms, is part of healthy communities as it gives people a sense of personal worth and provides the support needed to share ideas, agree objectives, develop plans and use others' strengths. You respect differences. You facilitate different contributions by a skilled 'process manager' who builds a supportive and effective team from a disparate group of individuals. You take action to avoid teams being riddled by destructive games, understanding that negative relationships destroy teamwork by undermining the quality of human support and generating defensiveness.

Component X: Maintaining upwards flow

If you have a high score on this component you are responsive, encouraging data to flow upwards so that you know what is going on. You receive communication from below. This means being in touch with all employees. Intelligence must be gathered so that potential problems and opportunities are well understood. You recognize that creative ideas often come from below. You gather data from below for five reasons: to collect information about strengths, weaknesses, opportunities and threats; to harvest ideas and creativity; to take the temperature of the organization; to be open to challenge; and to be seen to be responsive. You are convinced that valid and comprehensive information from the internal environment is essential for wise decision making.

Reproduced from *Developing Your People: Easy-to-use activities for improving management skills*
by Mike Woodcock and Dave Francis, Gower, Aldershot

Component XI: Fighting red tape

If you have a high score on this component you are efficient, not allowing excessively cumbersome and costly channels for communication. You know that channels of decision making and communication can become slow and inefficient; much unnecessary communication can take place. Tortuous and wasteful communication is 'red tape'; it consumes much time and generates frustration. 'Red tape' needs to be fought and defeated but, like weeds in a garden, it easily grows again!

Component XII: Demonstrating communication skills

If you have a high score on this component you are an effective communicator: you enable people to communicate well. You recognize that individual communication skills, both spoken and written, are the foundation of effective organizational communications. Individuals need to be able to express themselves effectively; otherwise mistakes occur, opportunities are missed, and poor decisions taken. You help to develop communication skills including: accurate self-perception, assertion, active listening, leadership, methodical approaches to problem solving and decision making, counselling, dealing with unconstructive people, trainer competency, creativity, writing skills and oral communication competency.

123

MACE action planning sheet

Consider your scores on the MACE questionnaire and discuss the results with another person.

Complete the activity by action planning as suggested below:

1. My personal communication strengths (high scores) are:

   a)

   b)

   c)

2. My personal communication development needs (low scores) are:

   a)

   b)

   c)

3. I could build on my strengths by:

DOING THESE THINGS MORE	DOING THESE THINGS BETTER

4. I could address my weaker communication skills by:

DOING THESE NEW THINGS	REDUCING OR STOPPING DOING THESE THINGS	DOING THESE THINGS MORE OR BETTER

125

Reproduced from *Developing Your People: Easy-to-use activities for improving management skills* by Mike Woodcock and Dave Francis, Gower, Aldershot

MANAGER'S AUDIT OF COMMUNICATION AND EFFECTIVENESS

I BEING SENSITIVE TO THE EXERNAL ENVIRONMENT

II HAVING A COMPELLING VISION

III BEING PERSUASIVE

IV CONSTRUCTING INTEGRATING MECHANISMS

V MANAGING THE PHYSICAL ENVIRONMENT

VI MAINTAINING DOWNWARDS FLOW

VII GENERATING TRUST

VIII COMBATING PREJUDICE

IX DEVELOPING TEAMS

X MAINTAINING UPWARDS FLOW

XI FIGHTING RED TAPE

XII DEMONSTRATING COMMUNICATION SKILLS

Reproduced from *Developing Your People: Easy-to-use activities for improving management skills*
by Mike Woodcock and Dave Francis, Gower, Aldershot

9

A personal skills inventory

Objectives

- To help managers to review their personal skills.

- To encourage managers to develop action plans to improve their personal skills.

Group size

The Personal skills inventory can be used by an individual working alone but is much more useful when two or three managers discuss their results together.

Time required

1 to 2 hours.

Materials required

1. One copy of Task sheet 9.1: Personal skills inventory for each participant.

2. OHP 9.1.

Description

To provide a framework for reviewing personal management skills.

	Method	Approx time
1	Introduce the exercise by saying that the inventory involves exploring personal characteristics and that participation is totally voluntary.	5 mins
2	Ask participants to complete Task sheet 9.1: Personal skills inventory and then, following the instructions, summarize the results.	15 mins
3	Finally, they review their results in discussion with others using the following format: Each person talks about the seven sections of the inventory (using OHP 9.1), telling the others why he or she ticked particular columns.	10 mins per participant
4	The others give feedback and try to identify a pattern in the answers.	10 mins per participant
5	After discussion, participants may make amendments and changes on the inventory.	10 mins
6	Each participant privately answers the question 'In what practical ways can I improve my problem-solving skills?' and writes down his or her answer.	10 mins
7	The discussion concludes with all participants sharing their ideas for improvement.	15 mins

Personal skills inventory

This inventory is designed to help you to assess your personal skills and identify areas for improvement. Answer each item as honestly as you can.

1. As you go through the inventory, put a tick for each item in the appropriate column. (Put two ticks if necessary.)

2. Fill in the blank spaces with any additional skills that are relevant to you.

3. Then go back over the list and circle three or four items that you feel it would be most useful to improve at this time. Write these priority items in the space provided.

	SKILLS I NEED TO IMPROVE	MODERATELY GOOD SKILLS	VERY GOOD SKILLS
Life/work balance			
1. Achieving balance in life and work.			
2. Taking time for physical health.			
3. Being close to loved ones.			
4. Remaining calm under pressure.			
5. Being satisfied with achievements.			
6. Finding spiritual contentment.			
7. (Also) _____			
Responsibility to the earth and others			
8. Minimizing exploitation of resources.			
9. Helping others to thrive.			

129

	SKILLS I NEED TO IMPROVE	MODERATELY GOOD SKILLS	VERY GOOD SKILLS
10. Being active in the community.			
11. Bringing beauty wherever I can.			
12. Showing respect to others.			
13. Enjoying achievement in all walks of life.			
14. Learning about the world.			
15. Avoiding prejudice.			
16. (Also) _____			
Achieving results			
17. Setting realistic objectives.			
18. Clarifying time limits.			
19. Setting measurable objectives.			
20. Ensuring that objectives are shared with others involved.			
21. Overcoming obstacles.			
22. Celebrating success.			
23. Breaking big tasks into chunks.			
24. Reviewing objectives regularly.			
25. (Also) _____			

Reproduced from *Developing Your People: Easy-to-use activities for improving management skills*
by Mike Woodcock and Dave Francis, Gower, Aldershot

	SKILLS I NEED TO IMPROVE	MODERATELY GOOD SKILLS	VERY GOOD SKILLS
Relating to others			
26. Listening to the feelings of others			
27. Showing empathy.			
28. Giving others confidence.			
29. Recognizing talent in others.			
30. Standing up for what I want.			
31. Co-operating in decision making.			
32. Keeping communication open.			
33. (Also) _____			
Being grounded			
34. Making time to be calm.			
35. Enjoying my own company.			
36. Listening to what I feel.			
37. Opening myself to energy from outside.			
38. Taking nourishment for the spirit.			
39. (Also) _____			

	SKILLS I NEED TO IMPROVE	MODERATELY GOOD SKILLS	VERY GOOD SKILLS
Learning			
40. Allowing new ideas to excite me.			
41. Admitting errors openly.			
42. Not desiring to be perfect.			
43. Accepting feedback from others.			
44. Building on my strengths.			
45. Taking time to learn.			
46. Teaching others.			
47. Exploring new ways of thinking.			
48. Applying what I've learned.			
49. (Also) _____			
Emotional expressiveness			
50. Expressing authentic emotions.			
51. Showing warmth.			
52. Satisfying deep desires.			
53. Being generous in giving energy.			
54. Finding inner strength.			
55. (Also) _____			

Priority items

Go back over the list and circle three skills that you feel it would be most useful for you to improve at this time. Write these below. Record practical suggestions to improve your skills in the final column.

Number	SKILLS FOR IMPROVEMENT	HOW I CAN IMPROVE
1.		
2.		
3.		

133

PERSONAL SKILL CATEGORIES

1. Life/work balance

2. Responsibility to earth and others

3. Achieving results

4. Relating to others

5. Being grounded

6. Learning

7. Emotional expressiveness

10

Unlocking creativity

Objectives

- To provide a framework for exploring personal creativity.

- To enable participants to begin exploring personal blockages to their creativity.

- To identify ways to develop personal creativity.

Group size

Six or more participants may undertake this activity.

Time required

Approximately 3 hours.

Materials required

1. Task sheet 10.1: The creative task.

2. Task sheet 10.2: Personal creativity audit

3. Task sheet 10.3: Personal creativity audit: scoring and interpretation.

4. Task sheet 10.4: Exercise.

5. OHPs 10.1–10.16.

135

6. Flipchart.

Description

To help participants experience unlocking sources of creativity.

	Method	Approx time
1	Introduce the activity by outlining the objectives and encouraging a spirit of openness and exploration during the process.	5 mins
2	Divide participants into groups of three to five and hand out copies of Task sheet 10.1: The creative task, which should be completed as directed.	30 mins
3	Each group then leads one or two other groups through the creative task they have designed.	20–30 mins
4	Hand out Task sheet 10.2: Personal creativity audit, and ask each participant to complete it privately.	5 mins
5	Give a short presentation on unlocking personal creativity, using the OHPs.	10 mins
6	Instruct participants to return to their original groups to score the Personal creativity audit, review the results using the Personal creativity audit: scoring and interpretation, and complete the Excrcisc as directed.	45 mins
7	Gather the participants together to review the activity and learn from the process. List comments on unlocking personal creativity on a flipchart and have then typed later to consolidate the learning from the session.	15 mins

The creative task

Directions

Your task is to devise an activity for other group(s) to undertake that will help the members to unlock their personal creativity. The activity must take no longer than ten minutes. You must provide all necessary instructions and materials. The personal safety of the members of the other groups must not be threatened. You have 30 minutes to prepare. Use the space below for note taking.

Personal creativity audit

Directions

Review your behaviour over the last hour. Answer the following items by circling the appropriate number.

1. I allowed myself to believe that I could be creative.

    Totally untrue   1   2   3   4   5   Totally true

2. I listened to my feelings.

    Totally untrue   1   2   3   4   5   Totally true

3. I looked at the problem from several different viewpoints.

    Totally untrue   1   2   3   4   5   Totally true

4. I built on the creative ideas of others.

    Totally untrue   1   2   3   4   5   Totally true

5   I did not immediately assess whether ideas were good or bad.

    Totally untrue   1   2   3   4   5   Totally true

6. I invested my energy in being creative.

    Totally untrue   1   2   3   4   5   Totally true

7. I used a flipchart (or another technique) to capture ideas.

    Totally untrue   1   2   3   4   5   Totally true

8. I did not accept the first idea that came along.

    Totally untrue   1   2   3   4   5   Totally true

9. I was comfortable while being uncertain.

    Totally untrue   1   2   3   4   5   Totally true

10. I enjoyed being part of a creative group.

    Totally untrue   1   2   3   4   5   Totally true

11. I was prepared to be open.

    Totally untrue   1   2   3   4   5   Totally true

12. I gave support to others.

    Totally untrue   1   2   3   4   5   Totally true

Reproduced from *Developing Your People: Easy-to-use activities for improving management skills* by Mike Woodcock and Dave Francis, Gower, Aldershot

13. I listened to others' ideas without evaluation.

Totally untrue   1   2   3   4   5   Totally true

14. I focused my attention on the task to be achieved.

Totally untrue   1   2   3   4   5   Totally true

15. I was willing to adopt other people's ideas.

Totally untrue   1   2   3   4   5   Totally true

Reproduced from *Developing Your People: Easy-to-use activities for improving management skills*
by Mike Woodcock and Dave Francis, Gower, Aldershot

Personal creativity audit: scoring and interpretation

Scoring directions

Transfer your scores from Task sheet 10.2: Personal creativity audit to the grid below. Share each group member's scores verbally or by creating the grid on a flipchart and posting each person's scores. Then complete the Exercise with your group.

ITEM	SCORE				
1. Belief in self-creativity	1	2	3	4	5
2. Listening to feelings	1	2	3	4	5
3. Varied viewpoints	1	2	3	4	5
4. Building on others' ideas	1	2	3	4	5
5. Suspension of judgement	1	2	3	4	5
6. Investment of energy	1	2	3	4	5
7. Use of techniques	1	2	3	4	5
8. Persistence	1	2	3	4	5
9. Comfort in uncertainty	1	2	3	4	5
10. Enjoyment of process	1	2	3	4	5
11. Openness	1	2	3	4	5
12. Giving support	1	2	3	4	5
13. Listening to others	1	2	3	4	5
14. Focused attention	1	2	3	4	5
15. Adopting others' ideas	1	2	3	4	5

Interpretation

A score of 4 or 5 indicates that you allow yourself to be personally creative. A score of 1 or 2 indicates that you hold back from letting your creativity flow. Below are comments on the 15 rated items.

1.	Belief in self-creativity	Creativity requires self-confidence and willingness to journey into the unknown.
2.	Listening to feelings	Feelings are often a source of insight and novelty.
3.	Varied viewpoints	Creativity requires the capacity to depart from conventional frameworks of the mind and play with ideas.
4.	Building on others' ideas	Ideas are rarely fully formed. Teamwork allows ideas to be built on.
5.	Suspension of judgement	Premature judgement inhibits the generation and exploration of ideas.
6.	Investment of energy	Without enthusiasm little of value will be achieved.
7.	Use of techniques	Creative techniques increase the capacity to develop ideas and transform them into innovations.
8.	Persistence	Creativity requires diligence, willpower and faith.
9.	Comfort in uncertainty	Ambiguity, uncertainty, and unknown difficulties can raise anxiety levels and act as inhibitors to the creative process.
10.	Enjoyment of process	Energy flows when we take pleasure in the creative process.
11.	Openness	Creativity thrives when people are willing to say what they think.
12.	Giving support	Creativity requires an element of risk taking. Support from others is nourishing and facilitates creativity.
13.	Listening to others	Input from people who think differently is a potent force for creativity.

141

Reproduced from *Developing Your People: Easy-to-use activities for improving management skills* by Mike Woodcock and Dave Francis, Gower, Aldershot

14. Focused attention — Without concentration the mind is less creative.

15. Adopting others' ideas — Willingness to 'sign up' for a good idea helps teams to be creative.

Exercise

Directions

With your group, answer the following questions for each group member in turn. Each individual should record on the worksheet the answers relevant to himself or herself.

1. What creative strength did I show in the activity?

STRENGTH	HOW SHOWN?
a)	
b)	
c)	

143

2.   What is hindering me from being creative?

HINDERING FACTORS	HOW SHOWN?	WHAT COULD BE DONE TO REDUCE OR ELIMINATE?

3. How could I strengthen my personal creativity?

IDEAS FOR STRENGTHENING CREATIVITY	HOW TO ACHIEVE?

UNLOCKING PERSONAL CREATIVITY

1. BELIEVE IN YOUR CREATIVE POTENTIAL
2. LISTEN TO YOUR FEELINGS
3. VIEW PROBLEMS IN DIFFERENT WAYS
4. BUILD ON OTHERS' IDEAS
5. DO NOT JUDGE IMMEDIATELY
6. INVEST YOUR ENERGY IN CREATIVITY
7. USE CREATIVITY TECHNIQUES
8. DO NOT ACCEPT THE FIRST IDEA
9. BE COMFORTABLE IN UNCERTAINTY
10. ENJOY YOUR CREATIVITY
11. BE OPEN – 'TELL IT LIKE IT IS'
12. GIVE SUPPORT TO THE CREATIVE IDEAS OF OTHERS
13. LISTEN TO THOSE WHO THINK DIFFERENTLY
14. FOCUS YOUR ATTENTION
15. ADOPT THE BEST IDEA (EVEN IF IT IS NOT YOURS)

Reproduced from *Developing Your People: Easy-to-use activities for improving management skills* by Mike Woodcock and Dave Francis, Gower, Aldershot

1. BELIEF IN SELF-CREATIVITY

Creativity requires self-confidence and willingness to journey into the unknown.

2. LISTENING TO FEELINGS

Feelings are often a source of insight and novelty.

3. VARIED VIEWPOINTS

Creativity requires the capacity to depart from conventional frameworks of the mind and play with ideas.

4. BUILDING ON OTHERS' IDEAS

Ideas are rarely fully formed.
Teamwork allows ideas to be built on.

5. SUSPENSION OF JUDGEMENT

Premature judgement inhibits the generation and exploration of ideas.

6.   INVESTMENT OF ENERGY

Without enthusiasm little of value will be achieved.

7. USE OF TECHNIQUES

Creative techniques increase the capacity to develop ideas and transform them into innovations.

8.   PERSISTENCE

Creativity requires diligence, willpower and faith.

9. COMFORT IN UNCERTAINTY

Ambiguity, uncertainty, and unknown difficulties can raise anxiety levels and act as inhibitors to the creative process.

10. ENJOYMENT OF PROCESS

Energy flows when we take pleasure in the creative process.

11. OPENNESS

Creativity thrives when people are willing to say what they really think.

12. GIVING SUPPORT

Creativity requires an element of risk taking. Support from others is nourishing and facilitates creativity.

Reproduced from *Developing Your People: Easy-to-use activities for improving management skills* by Mike Woodcock and Dave Francis, Gower, Aldershot

13.   LISTENING TO OTHERS

Input from people who think differently is a potent force for creativity.

14. FOCUSED ATTENTION

Without concentration the mind is less creative.

Reproduced from *Developing Your People: Easy-to-use activities for improving management skills* by Mike Woodcock and Dave Francis, Gower, Aldershot

15. ADOPTING OTHERS' IDEAS

Willingness to 'sign up' for a good idea
helps teams to be creative.

11

Personal paradigms questionnaire

Objectives

- To encourage individuals to assess their own 'mind-sets'.
- To facilitate the development of more creative management paradigms.

Group size

Unlimited.

Time required

Approximately 1 hour 20 minutes.

Materials required

1. Task sheet 11.1: Personal paradigms questionnaire, which includes scoring and explanation.

2. Task sheet 11.2: Exercise.

3. OHPs 11.1 and 11.2.

Method		Approx time
1	Introduce the activity and ask participants to complete Task sheet 11.1: Personal paradigms questionnaire.	15 mins
2	Give a brief introduction to the conceptual model using OHPs 11.1 and 11.2.	10 mins
3	Direct the participants to undertake the exercise given in Task sheet 11.2 in groups of three to five.	45 mins
4	Ask individuals to share their main learning from the session in open forum.	10 mins

Personal paradigms questionnaire

You are asked to compare two statements in relation to each other. You have three points to allocate between the two statements. Your points may be allocated as follows:

3		2		1		0
0	OR	1	OR	2	OR	3

1. I respond to circumstances and often reorganize. ☐ A

    I build formal and informal linkages across the organization. ☐ B

2. I believe that individuality is a great advantage. ☐ C

    I am constantly managing change. ☐ D

3. I systematically study customers' wants and needs. ☐ E

    I empower those who work for me. ☐ F

4. I reward ideas, even though they may not be practical. ☐ G

    I have a bias against systems and procedures. ☐ A

5. I build networks across the organization. ☐ B

    I measure the degree to which my work meets the needs of customers (internal and external). ☐ E

6. I coach my subordinates to increase their competence. ☐ F

    I ask people for their ideas. ☐ G

7. I recognize that different people possess special strengths. ☐ C

    I am constantly looking for new ways to satisfy customers. ☐ E

8. I remove as much 'bureaucracy' as possible. ☐ A

    I am never satisfied with current processes. ☐ D

9. I build communication links with many people. ☐ B

    I look upon ideas as an asset. ☐ G

10. I enjoy change. ☐ D

    I enlarge the scope of the jobs of my staff. ☐ F

Reproduced from *Developing Your People: Easy-to-use activities for improving management skills* by Mike Woodcock and Dave Francis, Gower, Aldershot

11. I work on the principle that organizations must always be flexible. ☐ A

I encourage people to be who they really are. ☐ C

12. I survey customers' needs (internal and external). ☐ E

I reward those who produce bright ideas. ☐ G

13. I 'contract' with others so that we have a win–win relationship. ☐ B

I always have a programme of charge to be managed. ☐ D

14. I encourage people to be open. ☐ C

I encourage my staff to take on more extensive tasks. ☐ F

15. I hold frequent planning meetings. ☐ A

I appraise my staff on the extent to which we meet customer requirements. ☐ E

16. I want people to think differently about their jobs. ☐ D

I receive many ideas from my staff. ☐ G

17. I frequently re-define objectives. ☐ A

I extend the scope of people's jobs. ☐ F

18. I extensively study what other companies are doing. ☐ B

I find debates constructive. ☐ C

19. I keep up-to-date with my specialism. ☐ B

I share information and responsibility. ☐ F

20. I will tolerate non-conventional behaviour from creative people. ☐ C

I value ideas for their own sake. ☐ G

21. I frequently set up teams to handle change projects. ☐ D

I formally report on the extent to which we satisfy our customers. ☐ E

Scoring the questionnaire

Add the scores for each letter and enter the total scores (letter by letter) below. The total should be 63.

☐ + ☐ + ☐ + ☐ + ☐ + ☐ + ☐

A   B   C   D   E   F   G   = 63

Analysis of the results

Take your scores for categories A to G and plot them on the graph below.

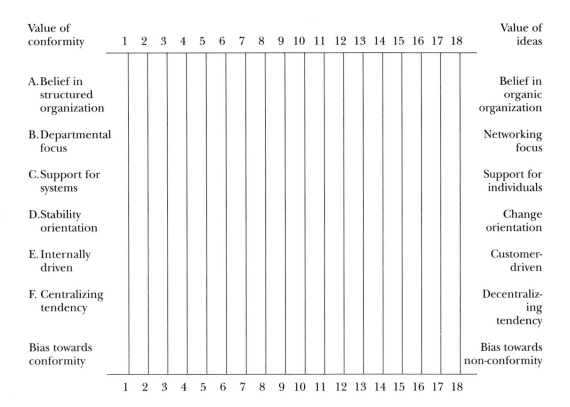

Explanation

A. *Structural assumptions*
    All of us carry a definition of a 'good' organization in our heads. For some a good organization is systematic, structured and ordered. Others see effective organizations as being fluid, organic and adaptable. More creative organizations need flexibility and a belief in organic organization.

B. *Focus*
    Every organization requires people to be specialists in their own areas. However, there is evidence that organizational creativity is enhanced by extensive communication; hence a network focus is necessary for a creative organization.

C. *Individualism*
    Organizational needs and systems define how individuals contribute to the organization. Creative endeavours require a much higher value to be placed on individuals whose lack of conformity must be seen as a potential source of strength.

D. *Change orientation*
    There are inherently different philosophies of change. Some people prefer incremental improvement and conservation whilst others prefer a radical programme of change which sweeps away what has been done before. A high change orientation increases creativity.

E. *Dedication*
    People's dedication varies. Some are concerned with internal factors such as process, conformity, organization and style. Others look outward for their inspiration, considering value added, competition and customer wants and needs. Creativity requires a strong dedication to the present and emerging needs of customers.

F. *Bias towards centralization*
    Organizations have to confront the dilemma of what to centralize. Power in the centre of an organization provides clarity and effectiveness but those in the centre can be overloaded, blinkered and uninformed. Decentralization brings advantages of widespread involvement in decision making but can lead to lack of focus and indecision. Creativity, if it is to be an organizational attribute, requires a degree of decentralization.

G. *Stance towards conformity*
    Conformity has many virtues. Each time you board an aeroplane imagine how you would feel if the maintenance crew were not compelled to conform to rules and procedures. However, excessive emphasis on conformity reduces creativity. Dedication to maintain

Reproduced from *Developing Your People: Easy-to-use activities for improving management skills*
by Mike Woodcock and Dave Francis, Gower, Aldershot

circumscribed behaviour reduces the probability that ideas will flourish.

This questionnaire provokes a discussion about the dominant 'management paradigm' being used by a manager. A management paradigm is a coherent set of beliefs which underlie behaviour.

Low scores suggest that the manager is using a 'traditional' set of beliefs about the nature of people and the nature of business. The organization is perceived to be a structure of formal roles. Precise planning and measured objectives provide necessary discipline. The individual is subsumed within the organization. Creativity is narrowly defined and a top–down hierarchical system is used for decision making. Such management paradigms are well-suited for predictable environments, especially in mature industries.

High scores suggest that the manager is using a 'new age' set of beliefs about the nature of people and the nature of business. The organization is perceived to be an ever-changing network of individuals structured around tasks of the moment. Long-term goals are avoided; instead there is a statement of direction and intent. The individual is highly prized. Argument, discussion and 'off the wall' innovation are welcomed.

Exercise

Consider your own profile. Where are you a strong leader of creativity? How could you further develop your creativity?

These are the situations in which I am a strong leader of creativity.	I could further develop my creativity in these situations.

Discussion questions

Reflect on the pattern of your scores shown and answer the following questions in discussion with others.

1. Is my dominant management paradigm 'traditional' or 'new age'?

2. What is the environment of my organization? How rapid is the rate of change?

Reproduced from *Developing Your People: Easy-to-use activities for improving management skills* by Mike Woodcock and Dave Francis, Gower, Aldershot

3. How appropriate is my current management paradigm for the organization at the present time?

4. How appropriate is my current management paradigm for the organization as it may change in the future?

5. What changes in my management skills and behaviour are desirable?

6. How might these changes be brought about?

7. How important is it to make these changes (i.e. shift my management paradigm)? Why?

8. What do I need to learn to sharpen my understanding of the importance of management paradigms?

1. MANAGEMENT PARADIGMS KEY QUESTIONS

A. How beneficial is system and structure?

B. Should your focus be on the team or whole organization?

C. Which is more important: the system or the individual?

D. Is constant change the desirable state?

E. How customer-driven are you?

F. Do you favour centralization or decentralization?

G. How valuable is conformity?

Reproduced from *Developing Your People: Easy-to-use activities for improving management skills* by Mike Woodcock and Dave Francis, Gower, Aldershot

2. 'Traditional' versus 'new age' paradigm

'TRADITIONAL' PARADIGM	'NEW AGE' PARADIGM
STRUCTURED	ORGANIC
DEPARTMENTAL	NETWORKING
SYSTEMATIC	INDIVIDUALISTIC
STABILITY-ORIENTED	CHANGE-ORIENTED
INTERNALLY DRIVEN	CUSTOMER-DRIVEN
CENTRALIZING	DECENTRALIZING

12

Blu cross

Objectives

- To provide a practical task which demands skilful research, creativity and teamwork.

- To develop individual creativity.

Group size

1. At least two groups should be involved, although any number of groups can participate at the same time.

2. Each group requires a separate room to work in and a complete set of materials.

3. Groups should have between four and seven members.

Time required

1 hour 30 minutes.

Materials required

The materials required are as specified in Task sheet 12.1.

Description

This is a practical task designed for use on training courses and team-building events. Prior to the activity find a balcony, window, or similar high point for the trials. This should be between 12 and 20 feet from the ground. The high point should be totally safe. It is useful if the facilitator can lightly score two diagonal lines in the form of a cross from corner to corner on each slab of Blu-Tack (see Task sheet 12.1: Blu cross instruction sheet). This acts as an aim point and assists in measurement later.

Method		Approx time
1	Introduce the task, allocate individuals to groups and ensure that groups begin the exercise described in Task sheet 12.1 at exactly the same time.	10 mins
2	Allow 40 minutes for preparation, following which the task takes place.	50 mins
3	When this is completed, the winner is announced, and the groups complete a process review, using Task sheets 12.2 and 12.3.	30 mins

Blu cross instruction sheet

In 40 minutes' time a sheet of Blu-Tack (approximately 5" x 3") will be positioned on the ground immediately below the designated balcony or window. Your team is asked to mark out a cross on the sheet of Blu-Tack. You have 40 minutes to prepare. The cross can be any size and points will be deducted for unevenness. You will have 5 minutes from start time to mark out your cross.

Rules

1. You may use only the materials provided.

2. The Blu-Tack must be unmarked by your group until the start signal is given.

3. Only members of the team at the designated balcony/window are permitted to play a role in the trials.

4. Nothing should be done which creates a safety hazard. Any team taking a risk will be disqualified immediately.

5. One of your team may be absent in the preparatory period to take measurements and so on.

Materials (for each group)

- 200 heavy duty elastic bands.

- 1 6-inch nail.

- 6-foot length of string.

- 1 ruler.

- 50 paperclips.

- 100 drinking straws (wider type).

- 1 box of Smarties or similar.

- 1 roll of sellotape.

- 3 packets of pipe cleaners.

- (One fresh slab of Blu-Tack to be available.)

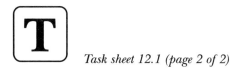

Measurement

A perfect cross is considered to comprise at least 13 boldly marked depressions as shown below:

For the first 13 boldly marked depressions on a correct line you will earn 10 points. For each additional depression on a correct line you will earn 3 points. (Note: correct means that part of the depression is within $^1/_4$ inch of a measured cross where the lines meet corner to corner.) Should you make fewer than 13 depressions you will lose 15 points for each missing depression. Depressions which are off the direct line (more than $^1/_4$ inch each way) are considered 'misses' and 5 points will be deducted for each miss up to 10 and then 20 points per miss thereafter.

$\boxed{\text{T}}$

Process review

Answer the following questions individually and then discuss them as a group using Task sheet 12.3.

1. How effectively did the group detect the key challenges of this task?

2. What process was used to generate ideas? How effective was it?

3. What process was used to select a solution? How effective was it?

4. What method was used to co-ordinate the group's efforts? With hindsight, are there any other methods of co-ordinating work?

5. How far was information from trials and experiments integrated into the design process?

6. What were the strengths of each individual in the group?

INDIVIDUAL	STRENGTHS

7. How could each individual contribute more or better?

INDIVIDUAL	IDEAS TO IMPROVE

8. What were the most satisfying aspects of the activity for you?

SATISFYING ASPECTS	WHY THEY WERE SATISFYING

T

9. What were the least satisfying aspects of the activity for you?

LEAST SATISFYING ASPECTS	WHY THEY WERE NOT SATISFYING

10. What would you personally do differently if you did the same exercise again?

NEW IDEAS	REASONS

Group review

Following the individual review, share the views of each group member and complete the analysis below.

If this group were undertaking a similar exercise again we would:

Do the following more or better ...	Do less or stop ...	Start doing ...	Continue doing ...

13

Learning style questionnaire

Objectives

- To heighten awareness of learning styles.
- To define one's own learning styles.
- To increase receptivity to learning from experience.
- To plan how to increase self-managed learning.

Group size

Any number.

Time required

1 hour 20 minutes.

Materials required

1. Task sheet 13.1: Learning style questionnaire.
2. Task sheet 13.2: Learning style questionnaire: scoring and interpretation.
3. Handout 13.1: Eight learning styles.
4. Task sheet 13.3: Exercise.

5.   OHPs 13.1–13.9.

Description

To help participants reflect on their approach to learning and plan how they can learn more effectively in the future.

Method		Approx time
1	Introduce the activity and invite participants to explore their own learning styles.	5 mins
2	Direct participants to complete Task sheet 13.1: Learning style questionnaire.	15 mins
3	Give a lecturette on the Eight learning styles, using the OHPs.	15 mins
4	Give each participant a copy of Task sheet 13.2: Learning style questionnaire: scoring and interpretation, Handout 13.1: Eight learning styles, and Task sheet 13.3: Exercise. Form participants into pairs to score the Questionnaire and to complete the Exercise as directed.	45 mins

Learning style questionnaire

Directions

Consider each questionnaire section and allocate 10 points among the eight statements to reflect what is important to you. You may distribute the points as you wish, but you must allocate all 10 points for each section. Record your points in the spaces provided.

Section One

Points

The moments in my life that have changed me the most have been...

A.　When others told how they felt about my conduct. _____

B.　When I have worked with an inspiring leader or expert. _____

C.　When I achieved a difficult target I thought I could not reach. _____

D.　When I was able to put confusing events into a theoretical framework. _____

E.　When I have been through a structured training programme. _____

F.　When I have attempted a new and different way of working. _____

G.　When other people have recognized and praised my successes. _____

H.　When something went wrong and I had to face my inadequacy. _____

Total ___10___

Section Two

My most important professional development experiences have been...

A.　Difficult projects that I successfully achieved. _____

B.　Obtaining a comprehensive, conceptual framework of management or of my profession. _____

C.　Being recognized as effective by my colleagues. _____

D.　Receiving comprehensive feedback on the impact of my behaviour. _____

E.　Throwing myself into completely new situations. _____

F.   Being inspired by watching more experienced managers/ professionals at work.   _____

G.   Failing to achieve something and reviewing where I went wrong._____

H.   Identifying the rules I should apply in predictable situations.   _____

                                                             Total   __10__

Section Three

In my current job the significant personal development experiences come from...

A.   Gaining confidence from the support of colleagues.   _____

B.   Succeeding despite severe difficulties.   _____

C.   Being told how others view my behaviour.   _____

D.   Adopting a structured approach to getting things done.   _____

E.   Watching how a more experienced manager or professional tackles similar tasks.   _____

F.   Learning from my mistakes.   _____

G.   Trying new ways of tackling situations.   _____

H.   Putting my experiences into a theoretical framework.   _____

                                                             Total   __10__

Section Four

As a manager or professional I gain most from...

A.   Structured approaches and checklists.   _____

B.   Honest feedback from others.   _____

C.   Observing an expert at work.   _____

D.   Gaining the support of co-workers.   _____

E.   Learning from my errors.   _____

F.   Theoretical models and frameworks.   _____

G.   Real challenges.   _____

H.   Trying a new approach.   _____

                                                             Total   __10__

Section Five

I would grow most in my job if I...

A.	Worked with an inspiring leader.	_____
B.	Gained confidence from being recognized by others.	_____
C.	Reviewed my mistakes.	_____
D.	Undertook a difficult new assignment.	_____
E.	Obtained new theoretical insights.	_____
F.	Tried new ways of tackling old problems.	_____
G.	Adopted a much more structured approach.	_____
H.	Obtained the views of others on my behaviour.	_____

Total   <u>10</u>

Learning style questionnaire: scoring and interpretation

Scoring directions

Transfer your scores from the five sections onto the grid below. Notice that the letters in each row are scrambled. Be careful to match your scores with the corresponding letters. Add the scores in each vertical column and enter the totals below.

SECTION								
ONE	A	E	D	F	C	H	G	B
SCORE								
TWO	D	H	B	E	A	G	C	F
SCORE								
THREE	C	D	H	G	B	F	A	E
SCORE								
FOUR	B	A	F	H	G	E	D	C
SCORE								
FIVE	H	G	E	F	D	C	B	A
SCORE								
TOTALS								
STYLES	FE	DI	CO	EX	AC	FA	RE	IN

Interpretation directions

Transfer the totals from the scoring grid to the chart below.

STYLE	YOUR SCORE	LEARNING STYLE
FE		FEEDBACK
DI		DISCIPLINE
CO		CONCEPTUALIZING
EX		EXPERIMENT
AC		ACHIEVEMENT
FA		FAILURE
RE		RECOGNITION
IN		INSPIRATION

- A high score indicates a preferred style of learning.

- With your group, review the Eight learning styles and then complete the Exercise.

Eight learning styles

1. **FEEDBACK**
   You learn from honest feedback from others about your behaviour. You need to know how others react to your way of operating. You listen to others and change your self-perception in the light of their viewpoints.

2. **DISCIPLINE**
   You learn by submitting yourself to disciplines and benefit from having structured approaches, checklists, and external organization. Once you have learned how to approach a situation, you follow established procedures.

3. **CONCEPTUALIZING**
   You learn from using a conceptual framework to simplify complexity. Once you understand basic principles, you gain confidence and feel able to 'distinguish the wood from the trees'. Your method of learning is intellectually challenging and you see theory as a vital guide to action.

4. **EXPERIMENT**
   You learn from trying new ways of tackling old problems. You like to try non-traditional methods and take care to review your experience. You are willing to take risks. 'Trial and error' describes your learning style.

5. **ACHIEVEMENT**
   You learn from undertaking challenge and overcoming real difficulties. Discovering that you can achieve provides confidence, insight, and new skills. You undertake new assignments without knowing how you will cope; you learn as you progress. The real world is your teacher.

6. **FAILURE**
   You learn by making errors and reviewing how you failed. The experience of things going wrong provides insight into your own inadequacy. Although this may cause you emotional distress, you overcome the setbacks and identify how you behaved inappropriately. This gives you the raw material to avoid the same situation in the future. You learn by recognizing and overcoming inadequacy.

7. **RECOGNITION**
   You learn from being accepted by others and receiving their approval. The support of others gives you strength and reinforces your self-image. You look to others to evaluate strengths and weaknesses.

8. **INSPIRATION**
   You learn by inspiration from competing experienced practitioners. Watching how they operate provides you with alternative models. Observing the styles of others gives you a variety of choices and you can emulate the best practice you see.

190

Reproduced from *Developing Your People: Easy-to-use activities for improving management skills* by Mike Woodcock and Dave Francis, Gower, Aldershot

Exercise

Directions

Answer the questions below. Then discuss your views with at least one other person.

1. What are your main learning styles?
   a.
   b.
   c.

2. What initiatives have you taken to manage your own learning in the last twelve months?

INITIATIVES	BENEFITS
a.	
b.	
c.	
d.	
e.	
f.	
g.	
h.	

3. What initiatives could you take to manage your learning further in the next twelve months? What could prevent you from taking these initiatives?

LEARNING INITIATIVES	POSSIBLE BARRIERS

4. What learning styles do not work for you and therefore might need to be developed?

a.

b.

c.

EIGHT LEARNING STYLES

- **LEARNING FROM INTERPERSONAL FEEDBACK**

- **LEARNING BY IMPOSED DISCIPLINE**

- **LEARNING BY ACQUIRING CONCEPTS**

- **LEARNING BY EXPERIMENT**

- **LEARNING BY ACHIEVING**

- **LEARNING FROM FAILURES**

- **LEARNING FROM OTHERS' RECOGNITION**

- **LEARNING BY BEING INSPIRED**

1.   FEEDBACK

You learn by feedback from others, by how others react to your way of operating. You listen to others and change your self-perception in the light of their viewpoints.

2.   DISCIPLINE

You learn by submitting yourself to
disciplines and benefit from having
structured approaches, checklists and
external organization. You follow
established procedures.

3. CONCEPTUALIZING

You learn from using a conceptual framework to simplify complexity. Once you understand basic principles, you gain confidence and feel able to 'distinguish the wood from the trees'. Your method of learning is intellectually challenging. You see theory as a vital guide to action.

Reproduced from *Developing Your People: Easy-to-use activities for improving management skills*
by Mike Woodcock and Dave Francis, Gower, Aldershot

4. EXPERIMENT

You learn from trying new ways of tackling old problems. You try non-traditional methods and review your experience. You take risks. 'Trial and error'.

5. ACHIEVEMENT

You learn from undertaking challenge
and overcoming difficulties.
Achievement provides confidence,
insight and new skills. You undertake
new assignments and learn as you
progress. The real world is your teacher.

Reproduced from *Developing Your People: Easy-to-use activities for improving management skills*
by Mike Woodcock and Dave Francis, Gower, Aldershot

6. FAILURE

You learn by making errors and reviewing. The experience of things going wrong provides insight. This may cause emotional distress but you overcome the setbacks and identify how you behaved inappropriately. You learn by recognizing and overcoming inadequacy.

7.   RECOGNITION

You learn from being accepted by others. The support of others gives you strength. You look to others to evaluate your strengths and weaknesses.

8. INSPIRATION

You learn by inspiration from competing
with experienced practitioners.
Observing styles of others gives you
choices and you emulate best practice.

14

Golden Sunshine Resort: a case study in management development

Objectives

- To learn how to use an analysis of a business situation to define management development needs.

- To reflect on techniques for personal development relevant to mid-career managers.

Group size

This activity is relevant to managers, training specialists and management teachers. There is no limit to the number of participants.

Time required

1 hour 15 minutes.

Materials required

1. Task sheet 14.1: Golden Sunshine Resort case study.

2. Task sheet 14.2: Personal development worksheet for each participant.

3. OHP 14.1.

Description

This activity provokes a discussion about techniques for management development.

	Method	Approx time
1	Divide participants into groups with three to five members and give each a copy of Task sheet 14.1: The Golden Sunshine Resort case study.	5 mins
2	Ask groups to read the case study and complete the exercise as directed.	35 mins
3	Invite groups to present their suggestions. OHP 14.1 may be shown.	15 mins
4	Direct participants to complete Task sheet 14.2: Personal development worksheet. It is helpful if they can discuss their self-assessment with a partner.	20 mins

The Golden Sunshine Resort case study

In September 1968 two men hired a helicopter and flew over the coastline of Northern Sicily. They were both property developers. Luigi Saloma was a tough entrepreneur who had spent his school days as a barefoot urchin in Mussolini's Rome whilst his friend, Solomon Goldfarb, had come from a wealthy family that had lost land, wealth, position and many lives during the Nazi persecution. They made a strange partnership – Luigi immaculately dressed in a $1000 suit whilst Solomon was short, squat and could never seem to buy a suit to fit him.

They flew over a deserted bay, majestic in its perfection and sparkling azure blue in the spring sunshine. Both men looked at each other. 'There,' they agreed in a glance.

Soon the land was bought and permission to build somehow obtained. The plan was to build a recreational complex with 43 villas, two hotels, bars, restaurants and a golf course. This was completed in 1972 and called the Golden Sunshine Resort.

A manager was hired to run the complex. He was Pierre D'Angle, a brilliant young Belgian national, who was an outstanding hotelier. Soon profits were rolling in and the two partners began other joint ventures.

As the years went by the Golden Sunshine Resort became more successful. The disposable income of middle-class people rose in Europe during the 1970s and 80s and much of this extra income was spent on leisure, holidays and so on. A new hotel was built on the complex and constant small improvements kept the resort fresh and exciting.

By the 1990s the situation began to change. Unemployment combined with an economic recession and rising taxes to squeeze the middle classes. Fewer people wanted to spend their time in a resort that was becoming increasingly polluted when the Seychelles, Florida and other new destinations became more affordable. Also other resorts, more modern and stylish, had been developed on the Sicilian coast. Where once Golden Sunshine had been a pioneer, the resort was now just one of many.

The partners met for their annual weekend at the resort, and, on the golf course, Solly said, 'I'm concerned about Pierre. He's been loyal and dedicated but he's 53 years old now and business is tougher than it's ever been. Pierre is a good man but I've got serious doubts about whether he's the right man to lead the resort for the next ten years.'

The two men played another hole and (as usual) Luigi won. Then the distinguished Italian said, 'For me loyalty is important. We owe Pierre. He's tried. He's been to conferences and got new ideas. He's taken full responsibility for the resort. He knows it like the back of his hand. We are the ones who have kept him from expanding – we were content with capital

Reproduced from *Developing Your People: Easy-to-use activities for improving management skills* by Mike Woodcock and Dave Francis, Gower, Aldershot

growth and a strong revenue stream. But I agree we now need someone to lead the business in a new direction. Everything needs to be rethought. We can spend big money if we believe in it and I would like Pierre to do it – if he's up to it.'

They walked on and joined Pierre in the clubhouse. Solomon said, 'Pierre, old friend, we've agreed that the resort has to be totally re-developed (something you've been telling us for years now). But both of us are concerned that you have been too sheltered all these years to lead the change. But we want to give you a chance. You've got a year to develop yourself. If you are then as good as the best we'll back you. Otherwise, you'll be side-lined.'

Pierre grinned. 'That's better than I thought,' he said. 'You've given me a chance.'

That evening Pierre sat in his favourite chair watching the sun ease its way into a blood-red sea and murmured to himself, 'I've got the chance to become a world-class resort manager and I know I've been too isolated here for years. But what do I do to develop myself?' Then Pierre recalled that a management seminar was taking place in one of the hotels and he went across and met a group of the experienced managers in the bar. He told them his story and asked for advice.

Your task

Assume that you are the group of managers to whom Pierre told his story. He has a year to develop himself. Reasonable funds can be made available. What should he do?

Personal development worksheet

If money and time were freely available, what five initiatives would you take to develop your management capability?

'IDEAL' INITIATIVES I WOULD TAKE	
a	
b	
c	
d	
e	

Now let's be practical. Take each initiative and decide what you can do, given the limits of your situation.

INITIATIVES	IN THE REAL WORLD, I COULD MAKE SOME PROGRESS BY TAKING THESE ACTIONS
a	
b	
c	
d	
e	

GOLDEN SUNSHINE RESORT

Eight experienced management development specialists discussed this case and recommended the following actions for Pierre D'Angle:

- A study tour of the world's best resorts.
- Two weeks with innovative resort architects – learning about their ideas.
- A short course on strategic marketing at a leading business school.
- Personal coaching from a social scientist on leisure trends in Europe.
- Attend the Harvard Business School short course on 'Managing Change'.
- Visit Japan to review developments in entertainment electronics.
- Spend three days working through a business plan for the resort with a leading strategy consultant.

Reproduced from *Developing Your People: Easy-to-use activities for improving management skills* by Mike Woodcock and Dave Francis, Gower, Aldershot

15

Personal visioning questionnaire

Objectives

- To provide a format for developing a personal vision.
- To clarify personal development needs.

Group size

There is no limit to the number of participants.

Time required

1 hour.

Materials required

1. Task sheet 15.1: Personal visioning questionnaire.

Description

This activity may be used for counselling, coaching or in a wide range of training situations.

Method		Approx time
1	Ask participants to complete Task sheet 15.1: Personal visioning questionnaire.	30 mins
2	Whenever possible participants should review their questionnaire with their boss or another person to clarify thinking and add additional ideas and perspectives.	30 mins

Personal visioning questionnaire

Answer each of the questions privately and then discuss the questionnaire to clarify and extend your ideas.

1. Which of your capabilities are you proud of?

I am proud of ...	For these reasons ...

2. What managerial capabilities does your organization want you to acquire?

My organization wants me to ...	For these reasons ...

3. Which of these do you feel able to achieve?

I am able to achieve ...	In these ways ...

4. Which of these do you feel unable to achieve?

I am unable to achieve ...	For these reasons ...

5.   What are your development needs in four key areas of management?

My development needs to improve financial performance are ...	My development needs to improve customer satisfaction are ...
My development needs to improve my organization are ...	**My development needs to increase the creativity of my organization are ...**

6. Over the next 5 years what new expectations or demands will be imposed on you by (a) the market place, (b) people within the organization, (c) people outside the organization?

NEW DEMANDS ON ME FROM		
Market	People in the organization	People outside the organization

7. From whom or what can you learn?

I can learn these things …	From these sources …

8.   What, in your opinion, should your personal development mission be?

My personal development mission is ...

9. How should your behaviour change over the next year?

MY BEHAVIOUR SHOULD CHANGE OVER THE NEXT YEAR	
From (present situation)	To (desired situation)

16

Stakeholder analysis

Objectives

- To clarify possible influencing strategies.
- To increase personal effectiveness.
- To develop 'political' skills.

Group size

1. This activity is particularly relevant for managers and supervisors who wish to make initiatives happen where they do not have direct control.

2. Any number of groups can take part at the same time.

Time required

1 hour.

Materials required

1. Handout 16.1: Stakeholder analysis.

2. Task sheet 16.1: Stakeholder analysis worksheet.

3. OHPs 16.1 and 16.2.

Description

The activity has been prepared in the form of a worksheet for use on 'real' issues but it can be used without adaptation for groups working on case studies or historical examples of successful or unsuccessful influencing strategies.

Method		Approx time
1	Give a brief input on stakeholder analysis using OHP 16.1 and OHP 16.2.	10 mins
2	Direct participants to read Handout 16.1: Stakeholder analysis and encourage them to ask questions to check their understanding.	10 mins
3	Break participants into natural teams or small groups (three to five people). Distribute Task sheet 16.1: Stakeholder analysis worksheet, and direct participants to complete it.	30 mins
4	Ask group members to summarize their learning. Emphasize key points on stakeholder analysis, re-showing OHP 16.1 and OHP 16.2.	10 mins

Stakeholder analysis

Background

A stakeholder is someone who:

- has power or influence.

- knows (or could know) what is going on.

- cares about the outcome.

- has definite wants and needs.

Understanding the wants and needs of stakeholders is important since 'success' can often be defined as 'satisfying as many of the stakeholders as possible to the greatest extent possible'.

Effective influencers:

- know all of the stakeholders.

- understand their wants and needs.

- influence the stakeholders towards their views.

- build bridges between stakeholders to reduce contrary pulls.

Four kinds of stakeholders

Stakeholders can be divided into four groups. The horizontal axis in Figure 16.1 represents the level of support you predict that each stakeholder will give. The vertical axis plots and predicts the magnitude of impact on the stakeholder.

The four groups are:

1. ALLIES – those who support the proposed change and are affected by it.

2. SUPPORTERS – those who support the proposed change but are not greatly affected by it.

3. BLOCKERS – those who oppose the proposed change but are not greatly affected by it.

4. HOSTILES – those who oppose the proposed change and are greatly affected by it.

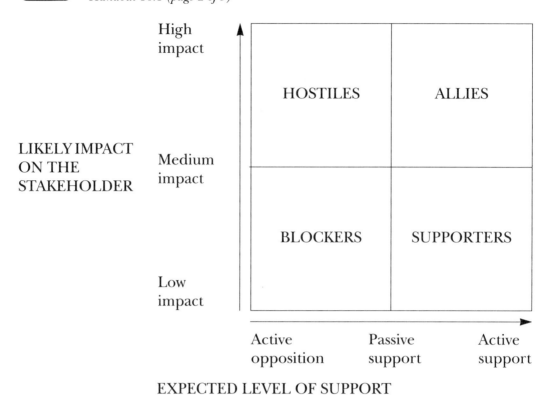

Figure 16.1

All four groups are equally important. Stakeholder analysis often requires a great deal of time. You need to understand their views and assess their flexibility. This reduces risk and builds support.

Positive stakeholders influence others in the direction you want to promote. Those not motivated to support you may express their negative perceptions and emotions in subtle or not so subtle ways: withdrawing energy, not releasing staff, missing meetings, offering no ideas and killing proposals.

Categories of stakeholders

1. *You:* You are a stakeholder, and the interest you demonstrate is important. If you invest your sustained commitment in a project it is more likely to succeed.

2. *Your team:* Your team's stake in success is significant. You need to ask yourself 'What hooks people in and builds team commitment?'

3. *Employees:* Employee groups are stakeholders in a full sense. What happens in the organization has a direct and pervasive impact on their lives. 'Opinion leaders', individuals with influence within the employee groups, are particularly important.

4. *Owners:* We can never ignore owners and shareholders. They have invested in the organization and have both rights and power.

5. *Suppliers and other business partners:* Suppliers and business partners are also stakeholders. Good suppliers care about performance because they recognize that their fortune depends on you.

6. *Customers:* We need customer input to direct our efforts. Somehow we have to find out what they need and what they don't need. This is made difficult because they may not know themselves, or, more frequently, have a partial view of their own wants and needs. The aim is to 'add value faster than cost'.

7. *Regulatory agencies:* Some government and non-government agencies or institutions have a significant role.

Mapping stakeholders' interests

There are four methods for discovering what stakeholders think and feel. These are:

● Interviews – helpful because they provide one-to-one data.

● Observation – adds value because observation is not dependent on people's perceptions.

● Questionnaires – best for large, dispersed groups.

● Focus groups – from five to eight individuals, conducted in one or two hours.

Stakeholder analysis worksheet

Before you progress further, define the change initiative that you wish to explore. Write a description in the box below:

The change initiative being studied is ...

---

1. Which 'senior' people could help the initiative? List as many as possible.

2. Select the three most influential people. Are they 'hostiles', 'blockers', 'supporters' or 'allies'? What is their current attitude to the initiative?

Person A's attitude is ...	Person B's attitude is ...	Person C's attitude is ...

3. Consider person A in relation to the initiative.

This would transform person A into a supporter or ally	This is the influencing strategy that has the greatest chance of success

4. Consider person B in relation to the initiative.

This would transform person B into a supporter or ally	This is the influencing strategy that has the greatest chance of success

227

Reproduced from *Developing Your People: Easy-to-use activities for improving management skills*
by Mike Woodcock and Dave Francis, Gower, Aldershot

5.   Consider person C in relation to the initiative.

This would transform person C into a supporter or ally	This is the influencing strategy that has the greatest chance of success

6. Apart from these people, who might influence the initiative? How can you win over *opinion leaders*?

Opinion leaders	Their motives	Strategies to win them over

7. Consider the sequence in which you should influence. Break down the process into steps. Draw a flow chart below.

INFLUENCING STRATEGY FLOW CHART

8. How should you behave to increase the chances of success?

To do	To avoid

Stakeholder analysis: summary

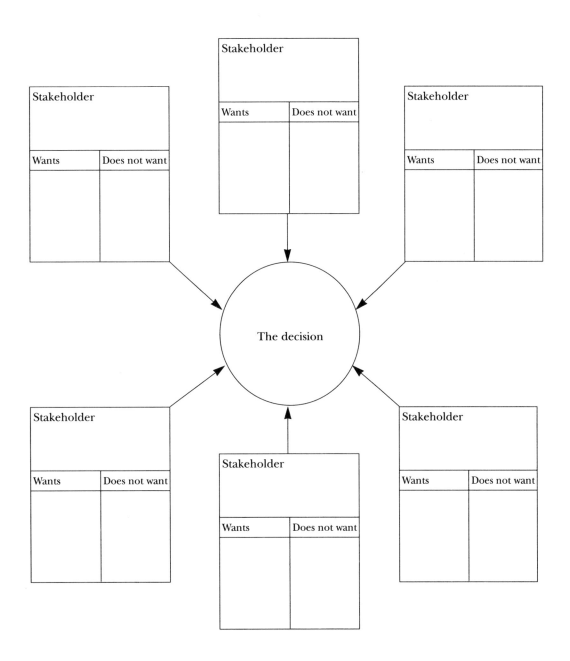

1. STAKEHOLDER ANALYSIS

Stakeholders are people:

- with power

- who care

- who can help or hinder the initiative.

Stakeholders' needs and wants must be understood.

- What do they want?

- What will they not accept?

- Which influencing strategies most likely to succeed?

Successful influencing requires:

- neutralizing 'hostiles'

- weakening 'blockers'

- strengthening 'supporters'

- honouring 'allies'.

2.   GROUPS OF STAKEHOLDERS

High impact		
	HOSTILES	ALLIES
LIKELY IMPACT ON THE STAKEHOLDER · **Medium impact**		
	BLOCKERS	SUPPORTERS
Low impact		

LIKELY IMPACT ON THE STAKEHOLDER

High impact — HOSTILES / ALLIES

Medium impact

BLOCKERS / SUPPORTERS

Low impact

Active opposition   Passive support   Active support

EXPECTED LEVEL OF SUPPORT

The four groups are:

1.   ALLIES – those who support the proposed change and are affected by it.

2.   SUPPORTERS – those who support the proposed change but are not greatly affected by it.

3.   BLOCKERS – those who oppose the proposed change but are not greatly affected by it.

4.   HOSTILES – those who oppose the proposed change and are greatly affected by it.

17

Problem solving using Force Field Analysis

Objectives

- To teach a technique for analysing a complex problem.

- To deepen understanding of the relative strength of forces which impact on a situation.

- To provide a basis for planning a multi-dimensional change programme.

- To introduce a team problem-solving tool.

Group size

Any number of groups with three to seven members.

Time required

1 hour 15 minutes (minimum).

Materials required

1. Handout 17.1: Problem solving using Force Field Analysis.

2. Task sheet 17.1: Force Field Analysis.

3. Task sheet 17.2: Using Force Field Analysis for real.

4.   OHPs 17.1 and 17.2.

Description

A step-by-step approach to solving a problem by using one of the most effective problem-solving tools available.

Method		Approx time
1	Present the core concepts of Force Field Analysis using OHPs 17.1 and 17.2 and talk through Handout 17.1: Problem solving using Force Field Analysis.	15 mins
2	Divide participants into trios or pairs. Invite each to select one change objective which is then worked through using the procedure described in Handout 17.1 and Task sheet 17.1.	45 mins per person
3	Gather participants to review the experience and complete Task sheet 17.2: Using Force Field Analysis for real.	15 mins

Problem solving using Force Field Analysis

Force Field Analysis is a conceptual tool for studying a situation that you want to change. The method was first described by Kurt Lewin[1] and is based on the observation that, at a moment in time, any situation can be described as a balance between two types of forces. These are 'helping forces' which facilitate movement wanted by the change agent and 'hindering forces' which oppose movement wanted by the change agent, as shown in Figure 17.1.

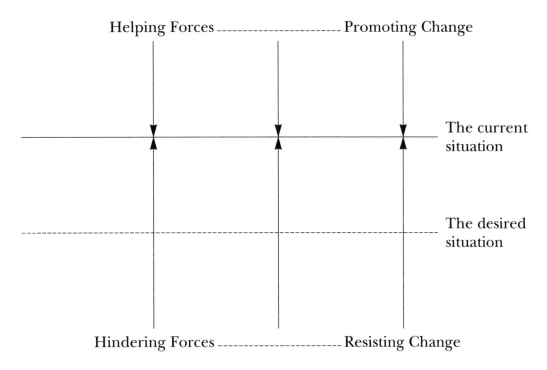

Figure 17.1

It may help you to imagine the helping forces as 'balloons' and the hindering forces as 'weights'.

What to do

Force Field Analysis is a tool for those who want to facilitate change. The first step is to clarify what changes you want to see (that is, describe the 'ideal' situation). Try to define the changes you want to see happen as precisely as

---

1. Kurt Lewin, 'Frontiers in Group Dynamics: I. Concept, Method, and Reality in Social Sciences: Social Equilibria and Social Change', *Human Relations*, 1947, 1(1), pp. 5–41.

possible. When you want to facilitate a multi-dimensional change process it may be necessary to consider each dimension separately.

When you have decided on the changes you want to initiate, the forces on both sides must be identified. Then they must be weighed in terms of the amount of force they exert. When we can define clearly what these various forces are and how significant (or strong) they are, there is a better chance of bringing about change in the direction we seek.

We can bring about change in three ways: by increasing the forces prompting change, by adding new forces, or by reducing the forces resisting change. The most effective way is to add to the driving forces and, at the same time, to weaken the resisting forces.

Select a change need that you consider important. If possible, it should be a situation that has given you cause for concern and that, if changed, would lead to significant improvement. Choose an issue for which a solution is possible, though difficult. Then work through the following steps, using Task sheet 17.1.

1. Identify the change need as you see it now and describe it in writing.

2. Define the change need in terms of (a) the present situation and (b) the situation you would like to see.

3. Make a list of the forces working against your desired change (hindering forces) and a list of the forces working for the change (helping forces). These forces can be related to people, resources, time, external factors, and so on – anything that could hinder or help you to make a change. When identifying forces, it is helpful to be specific and to draw a force field diagram.

4. Rank each force in terms of its strength.

5. For each hindering force identified, list the actions you could take that might reduce or eliminate the force.

6. For each helping force identified, list the actions you could take that might increase the force.

7. Consider whether you could add new helping forces.

8. Determine the most promising steps you could take towards achieving desirable change and identify the resources available to help you.

9. Re-examine your steps and put them into a sequence, omitting any that do not seem to fit your overall goals.

10. Set yourself milestones so that you can assess your progress.

Force Field Analysis

Directions

Work through the Task sheet step by step, discussing each section with a small group of colleagues to clarify your thinking.

1. The change needed ...

   This is what I/we want to achieve ...

   The reasons why whis change is important are ...

2a. The present situation is ...

2b. The desired situation is ...

3a.   The forces which are helping me are …

3b.   The forces which are hindering me are …

4. This is my analysis of the helping and hindering forces now. The relative strengths of the forces are shown by chevrons.

Helping forces

Present situation

Desired situation

Hindering forces

241

5. How can I weaken the hindering forces?

6. How can I strengthen the helping forces?

7. How can I add new helping forces?

8.   These I could do ...

9.   This is my plan

10.   This is how I will monitor progress

Using Force Field Analysis for real

Now fill out this further worksheet (it only takes 3 minutes!) to help you plan how to use Force Field Analysis on real issues.

These are situations that would be helped if I used Force Field Analysis

It would be helpful to involve these people

My plan is ...

1. Example Force Field Diagram

Problem: To reduce the scrap rate in an engineering department.

Helping forces – tending to reduce scrap rate

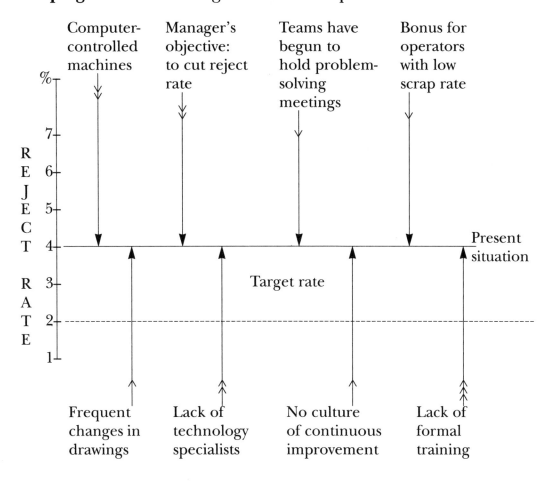

Hindering forces – tending to increase scrap rate

Note

● Change need (reduce the reject rate from 4% to 2%) clearly specified.

● Strength of forces shown by chevrons.

245

Reproduced from *Developing Your People: Easy-to-use activities for improving management skills* by Mike Woodcock and Dave Francis, Gower, Aldershot

2. TEN STEPS FOR USING FORCE FIELD ANALYSIS

1. Specify the change need.

2. Define the 'present' and 'ideal' situation.

3. List helping and hindering forces.

4. Rank the strength of each force.

5. Explore how to weaken hindering forces.

6. Explore how to strengthen helping forces.

7. Ask 'can I add new helping forces?'

8. Decide on your initiatives.

9. Put your actions into a plan.

10. Define how you will check progress (milestones).

18

'If you don't measure it you are only practising ...'

Objectives

- To deepen managers' understanding of the impact of measures of performance.
- To develop skills in formulating a 'balanced scorecard' approach to measurement.

Group size

Unlimited.

Time required

1 hour.

Materials required

1. Handout 18.1: The Elspeth Jordan case study.

2. Task sheet 18.1: Your task.

3. Task sheet 18.2: My measures worksheet.

4. OHPs 18.1 and 18.2.

Description

This activity is designed to raise consciousness about performance management in a business. It is designed for all levels of management and may also be used as a student exercise.

Method		Approx time
1	Introduce the session by giving an overview of the importance of measures using OHP 18.1: Measures.	5 mins
2	Divide participants into groups of four to seven and give out Task sheet 18.1: The Elspeth Jordan case study, and Task sheet 18.1: Your task. This should be completed as directed.	25 mins
3	Take a presentation from each group (playing the role of Elspeth Jordan). To complete this section of the activity, show OHP 18.2 which illustrates one way of measuring McDove Portugal.	15 mins
4	Return participants to their groups to complete Task sheet 18.2: My measures worksheet as directed.	15 mins

The Elspeth Jordan case study

Elspeth Jordan is the Vice-President in charge of the Portuguese division of McDove Consulting. She has 27 staff (3 principal consultants, 10 consultants, 5 junior consultants, an office manager, a marketing manager and 7 administrative staff).

McDove is an American consultancy specializing in strategy, human resource management, operations, logistics, information technology and product development. Over the past 30 years McDove have expanded internationally and now have country divisions in most countries of the world.

McDove has a new President, Miriam Coot, and she has been greatly influenced by recent developments in management theory springing from the Harvard Business School. In particular, Miriam believes that it is imperative to develop a comprehensive measuring system so that everyone works to clear guidelines. Recently she sent this memo to all national Vice-Presidents:

FROM: M Coot
TO: National VPs
SUBJECT: Measurement

I believe that we do what we are measured upon and fail to do that which is unmeasured. I want to agree a comprehensive set of measures which will apply to all national divisions. Each national VP will submit to me a list of the 10 key areas that they feel should be measured to give an accurate rounded assessment of performance. I will select the 7 I feel give a balanced scorecard and inform you all.

Please return your list of proposed measures on 1 sheet of paper by the month end.

Signed in her absence

Henry Sparrow
Secretary to M Coot

Elspeth sat musing at her desk. She agreed with the principle that key performance indicators should be measured, but which ones would give a balanced assessment which would comprehensively, realistically and fairly evaluate both present capability and future potential?

She began to make a list of possible measures, beginning with the obvious financial measures and then moving on to more complex but equally vital indicators of the health of the consultancy. Before long there were 40 possible measures on her pad and a new one came every 30 seconds. Items included:

- Profit before tax

- Client numbers

- Client satisfaction

- Staff turnover

- New customers signed up

- New services developed

- Staff capability

- Cost per day

- and so on …

Elspeth paused. Before long there would be 100 possible measures but no evaluation of their usefulness.

Perhaps, she reflected, she could categorize the measures and pick out those which were important. But how to establish the categories? Should they be related to today's performance or McDove's longer-term strategic objectives?

This would need more thought, she decided. Perhaps she was too close to the business. Then an idea struck. Why not ask a panel of outsiders who knew the business world to spend half an hour thinking about the question and elicit their opinion? After all, any manager ought to be able to give an opinion on the measures that should be used to evaluate the performance of a national consulting business.

Your task

Assume that your group is a panel set up to advise Elspeth Jordan. What 10 measures do you think should be used? Make sure that the indicators you suggest can be objectively measured.

My measures worksheet

If I were the chief executive of the organization, I would want to measure the following 10 indicators of performance by the holder of my current job.

PERFORMANCE MEASURES	REASONS MEASURED	HOW THIS CAN BE DONE
1		
2		
3		
4		
5		
6		
7		
8		
9		
10		

1. MEASURES

- Measures greatly affect behaviour.

- Areas not measured cannot be managed systematically

- Measures need to be objective.

- Measures must include how things are done (process) as well as what is achieved (outcomes).

- The aim is to select a portfolio of measures (a 'balanced scorecard') which give a valid assessment.

2. A BALANCED SCORECARD FOR A CONSULTING COMPANY

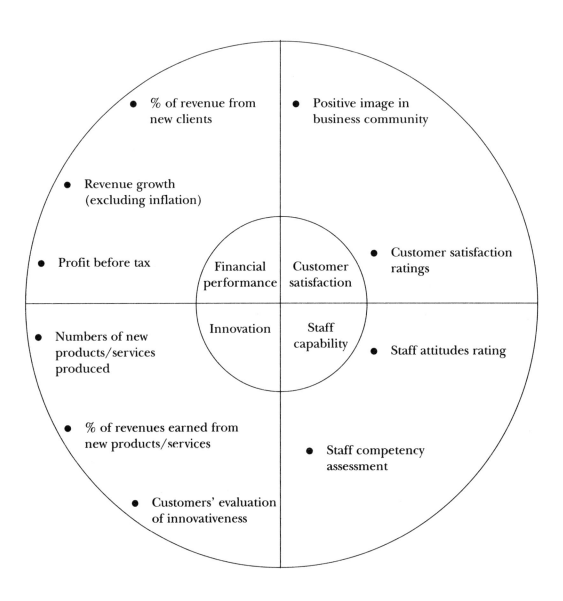

19

Tiers of objectives

Objectives

- To provide a technique that assists in the clarification of objectives.

- To improve communication processes in objective-setting situations.

- To develop skills in discriminating between different levels of objectives.

- To demonstrate the link between objective setting and task definition.

Group size

The activity is best undertaken by a small group (between 3 and 6 members) and may be used in formal training situations when several groups work under the supervision of a trainer.

Time required

Approximately 1 hour.

Materials required

1. Each group will require a room to work in.

2. Prepared post-it notes (see below).

3. A large white board. In the absence of a white board, the post-its can be

laid out on a long table.

4. Handout 19.1: Tiers of objectives.

5. Task sheet 19.1: Tiers of objectives: task.

6. Task sheet 19.2: Tiers of objectives: review.

7. OHP 19.1.

Description

Tiers of objectives is a simple, profound but subtle technique that can be learned quickly. This activity clarifies the principle and gives an opportunity for skill development.

Statements to be written on post-it notes

Copy each of the 30 statements below in large letters with a felt pen on to post-it notes. Only one statement is written on each post-it note. One complete set of 30 post-its is required for each participating group.

- Put 3 new rubbish bins in the school play area by March 15.

- Develop strong co-operation with the parents of our school children.

- Increase the percentage of children passing the basic examination in computer programming.

- Improve the quality of our Education for Leisure course.

- Prevent unwelcome strangers from coming on to the school property.

- Review the school's education philosophy.

- Replace the broken tap in cloakroom C.

- Maintain and improve a progressive educational institution.

- Get 1000 people to attend the school play this year.

- Improve our record of examination successes.

- Recruit a replacement cleaner by April 1.

- Obtain a new hamster exercise wheel by March 1 for Tom (the hamster).

- Give better career guidance for children who are finishing school.

- Buy a copy of *Managing Your Own Career* for library within 1 month.

- Arrange for training in career counselling for selected teachers.

- Give all fifth-year students a 2-hour career counselling session.

- Produce by Thursday a poster advertising the school play.

- Buy another computer for the computer lab.

- Improve security and building maintenance in the school.

- Improve the care of school pets.

- Employ an ex-actor by May 1 to coach pupils in the school play.

- Publish the school's examination results for parents.

- Arrange a series of staff meetings to address questions of educational philosophy.

- Circulate a copy of *New Thinking in Teaching* to all members of staff.

- Improve the quality of school equipment.

- Develop a training programme for new school cleaner.

- File hamster's claws.

- Establish rota for teachers to patrol school yard.

- Study *Best Buys in Computers* magazine.

- Complete an audit of repairs needed to school equipment.

Method		Approx time
1	Give each participant a copy of Handout 19.1 and ask them to read it – after which generate a short discussion to ensure that the principles are understood.	15 mins
2	Give groups a set of prepared post-its and a copy of Task sheet 19.1.	15 mins
3	Following the activity, ask group members to reflect on their experience for 15 minutes and discuss how the Tiers of objectives technique can be used to improve practical communication. Task sheet 19.2 provides a structure for this discussion.	15 mins
	If relevant, show OHP 19.1, which provides guidance for using the technique.	15 mins

Tiers of objectives

An objective is a statement that describes something to be achieved in the future. The Oxford Dictionary defines it in military terms as 'the point to which an advance of troops is directed'. The essence of an objective is that it defines where we want to go without describing how we are going to get there.

Without objectives people do not know where to invest their time or resources, and they drift in an uncoordinated way. If purpose and a sense of meaning are lost, then commitment diminishes. When objectives are unclear it is impossible to make effective plans or allocate tasks.

Despite the obvious importance of objectives, many people find it difficult to set them. Why is this? Let's review a few statements of business objectives:

● To make a net profit of 10 per cent for distribution to shareholders.

● To ensure that all customer queries are answered within 24 hours.

● To bring out one successful new product each year.

● To reduce by 10 per cent the number of paperclips used in the finance department by March 1.

Each of the above statements is an objective; each states a 'point to which an advance is directed'. Moreover, the objectives are consistent with each other. For example, reducing the number of paperclips consumed by the finance department may well make a small contribution to the overall objective, which is corporate profitability.

However, look at the four examples again and ask, 'Where do they differ?' A close examination reveals that the real difference is in their degree of generality or specificity. Making a profit is a broad and general goal, whereas saving paperclips and answering customer queries are narrow and specific objectives that give a clear indication of exactly what will have to be done. The objective 'to bring out one successful new product each year' is intermediate; it sets a clear point for advance but many short-term and specific objectives will have to be formulated to achieve this.

Looked at from a logical point of view, objectives can be arranged in tiers with the broadest at the top and the most specific at the bottom. It is important to make this distinction because broad objectives are too general to be implemented immediately and specific objectives only make sense if they serve a wider goal.

We arrange objectives in tiers by looking at each and asking: 'It this a concrete and limited statement or a broad, far-sighted goal?' The question 'Is this a statement of why or how?' makes the distinction clearer. 'Why' objectives are broad, whereas 'how' are specific.

Reproduced from *Developing Your People: Easy-to-use activities for improving management skills*
by Mike Woodcock and Dave Francis, Gower, Aldershot

When we draw a chart of tiers of objectives, a pyramid shape emerges as shown in the air travel example (Figure 19.1).

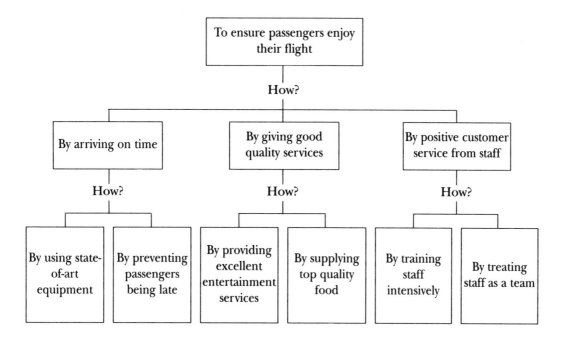

Figure 19.1

Here we have three tiers only – as you study the diagram note how the objectives become more specific lower down the chart. Of course, many more specific objectives would need to be developed – each one leading to an action programme but logically related to the broad objective at the top (sometimes called 'the aim').

Tiers of objectives: task

You will be issued with a set of post-it notes. Each has a written objective which was prepared by the teachers of a school. You should work with the other members of your group and, by consensus, arrange the objectives in tiers with the broadest at the top and the most specific at the bottom.

Move the post-its around until you are satisfied with the result. You have 15 minutes for this task.

Tiers of objectives: review

Spend a few minutes answering the questions below and then discuss your comments with other members of your group. You have 15 minutes to complete the review.

1. What have you learned about setting objectives from this exercise?

2. What levels of objectives are you given in your work?

3. What levels of objectives do you set for others in your work?

Task sheet 19.2 (page 2 of 2)

4.   How can the Tiers of objectives concept be used in your work?

POSSIBLE APPLICATIONS	HOW TO USE THE TECHNIQUE

TIERS OF OBJECTIVES

WHAT TO DO

1. Write the broad objective (aim) on a post-it. Place at the top of a board.

2. Ask 'How?'. Write each idea on a post-it, expressed as an objective.

3. Continue until specific objectives (tasks) are identified on bottom tier.

4. Eliminate duplications.

5. Put specific objectives into a task action plan.

20

Team visioning

Objectives

- To show team or departmental managers how to develop a practical vision to guide group development.

- To offer a format to relate team/department visions to the business vision.

- To explore the importance of visioning as part of the team development process.

- To provide a format for launching a new project team.

Group size

1. This activity is designed for managers with their own teams or departments.

2. It is most relevant for middle level managers or project leaders – those who control a defined department or sub-unit within an organization.

3. The activity may be adapted for use on training programmes, perhaps as part of a structured action learning programme.

4. As many participants as desired may take part at the same time.

Time required

1 hour 50 minutes.

Materials required

1. Task sheet 20.1: Team visioning worksheet.

Description

To provide a team with the opportunity to work together and develop a shared vision of their mission, strategy and core values.

Method		Approx time
1	Introduce the activity by outlining the objectives and discussing its purpose.	5 mins
2	Ask participants to complete Task sheet 20.1: Team visioning worksheet privately.	45 mins
3	Invite participants to meet under the direction of the team leader. Each question is worked through in turn. Encourage participants to share their views openly. A consensus should be reached for each item.	1 hour

Team visioning worksheet

Directions

You are about to undertake a project to review the work of your team. This is not a theoretical exercise; the conclusions will be real and should guide the way that you work in the future. First, each individual should complete the worksheet privately. Then work through the 10 items as a team, ensuring that you clarify each item before you move on. Be thorough – nothing will be gained if you rush the process.

Answer the 10 questions in order.

1. What are the reasons for the existence of your team? Answer this question by saying what outputs you supply (products or services to other teams, departments or customers). Rank the 'outputs' in order of importance.

    Outputs supplied

    a.

    b.

    c.

    d.

    e.

2. Now think about your 'customers' (the receivers of the outputs you supply to other teams, departments or end users).

   Who are your customers?

   What do they want from you?

   How successful are you in meeting your customers' needs?
   Marks out of 10   ☐

3. What do you think engenders a sense of pride in the people who work in your department? Rank order the items.

These are current sources of pride	These should be sources of pride
a.	
b.	
c.	
d.	
e.	

4. What are the 'blockages' which prevent your department from being excellent?

Blockages to excellence	Effect on performance
a.	
b.	
c.	
d.	
e.	

5. Generate a 25–50-word vision statement for your team.

   OUR TEAM VISION IS ....

6.   From the vision statement you have just written analyse:

What we will strive to do

What we will not do

We will measure our success in these ways

7. Identify the reasons why the people in your team should 'buy into' this vision statement.

Item in vision statement	Why team members should 'buy in'

8. Identify the reasons why your customers will benefit from the implementation of your vision statement.

Item in vision statement	Why this will benefit our customers

9. How does this vision statement link to the company's vision?

Item in vision statement	Link with company vision statement

10. How should you go about implementing the changes needed to implement your vision?

Changes needed	How to manage the changes	How we can measure success

21

'Boom' objectives

Objectives

- To demonstrate a simple way to improve the quality of objective setting.
- To facilitate appraisal and development reviews.
- To suggest practical ways of improving skills in setting objectives.

Group size

Any number of groups with three to seven members.

Time required

1 hour.

Materials required

1. Task sheet 21.1: Objective-setting questionnaire.
2. Task sheet 21.2: review worksheet.
3. Task sheet 21.3: 'Boom' objectives worksheet.
4. OHP 21.1.

Description

An easy way to set powerful objectives.

Method		Approx time
1	Introduce the activity and invite participants to complete Task sheet 21.1: Objective-setting questionnaire.	15 mins
2	Direct participants to meet in pairs to reflect on the results of their questionnaire using Task sheet 21.2: Review worksheet and develop a checklist of improvement ideas.	15 mins
3	Give an introduction to the 'Boom' method of writing individual objectives using OHP 21.1.	15 mins
4	Ask participants to complete Task sheet 21.3: The 'Boom' objectives worksheet and discuss it in pairs.	15 mins

Objective-setting questionnaire

Complete the checklist by circling a numner on each line where appropriate, then total your scores at the bottom.

I never discuss objectives with my subordinates.	0 1 2 3 4 5	I always discuss objectives thoroughly with my subordinates.
My objective-setting sessions are a year or more apart.	0 1 2 3 4 5	Sessions to update objectives are held every three months or more frequently.
I set objectives for achievement of project goals only.	0 1 2 3 4 5	I set objectives for financial performance, customer satisfaction, organization development and innovation.
I rarely clarify how we are going to measure success.	0 1 2 3 4 5	I ensure that tangible measures of success are agreed on.
We rarely meet to discuss performance.	0 1 2 3 4 5	I ensure that we meet regularly to discuss performance.
Once set, objectives are rarely changed.	0 1 2 3 4 5	Objectives are open to renegotiation when situations change.
I specify only the duties/ responsibilities of subordinates.	0 1 2 3 4 5	I ensure that my contribution is clearly identified.
Unachievable objectives are often set.	0 1 2 3 4 5	Objectives can almost always be achieved.
We rarely check the organizational relevance of individual objectives.	0 1 2 3 4 5	Individual objectives are checked to ensure organizational relevance.
No steps are taken to ensure that people share information about their objectives.	0 1 2 3 4 5	We take steps to ensure that people share information about their objectives.

Total _____

275

Scoring

- Most managers score between 30 and 40 points.

- A higher score indicates a systematic approach to objective setting.

- A lower score suggests insufficient skill or insufficient attention to objective setting.

Review worksheet

Complete the chart below.

Criteria for effective objective setting	Ways in which I can improve
1. Through discussion with subordinates.	a. b. c.
2. Objectives updated frequently.	a. b. c.
3. Performance assessed by 'balanced scorecard' of objectives.	a. b. c.
4. Clear criteria for judging success.	a. b. c.
5. Regular meetings to discuss performance.	a. b. c.

Reproduced from *Developing Your People: Easy-to-use activities for improving management skills* by Mike Woodcock and Dave Francis, Gower, Aldershot

Criteria for effective objective setting	Ways in which I can improve
6. Flexibility when circumstances change.	a. b. c.
7. Responsibilities of all specified.	a. b. c.
8. Achievable objectives.	a. b. c.
9. Link between personal and organizational objectives clarified.	a. b. c.
10. Clear communication about objectives of all involved.	a. b. c.

'Boom' objectives worksheet

Consider your own job and, as an exercise, write one 'Boom' objective in each box below. Identify the way that this will be measured and write a description in the 'measurement tool' box. All objectives should follow the 'Boom' formula.

A 'Boom' objective is **B**usiness-based, **O**utput-specific, **O**wned and **M**easurable.

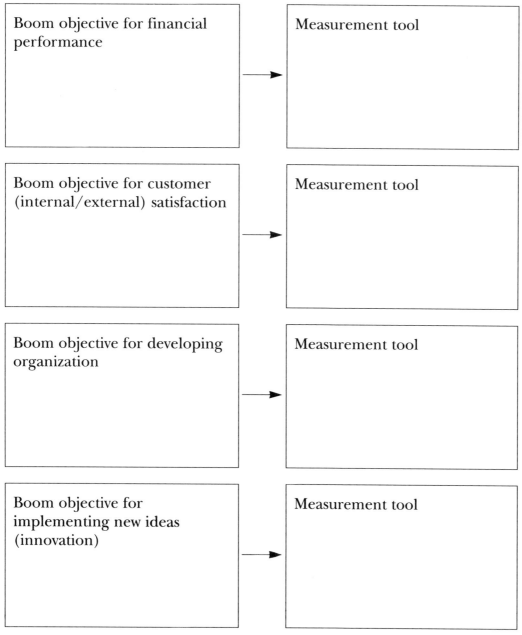

Later your should complete the exercise by listing all your objectives in each category.

'BOOM' OBJECTIVES

All objectives should be:

Business-based
(directly related to company goals)

Output-specific
(say *what* will be achieved, not *how*)

Owned
(a specific person or group is held accountable)

Measurable
(so that performance can be objectively assessed)

Example: To reduce cleaning costs in factory A by 10% as compared with last year by 31 March (Albert Tidy to lead project).

22

The failure workbook

Objectives

- To give feedback on dimensions of management style which reduce effectiveness.

- To sharpen understanding of the reasons why initiatives fail.

- To improve project management skills.

- To allow individuals to consider how far their own behaviour contributes to failure.

- To contribute towards developing a culture of learning from experience within the organization.

Group size

1. Any number of groups with between three and seven members can take part at the same time.

2. The exercise has proved especially useful when a group of managers from a single organization gets together to discuss projects or initiatives which have 'gone wrong'!

Time required

1 hour 30 minutes.

Materials required

1. Task sheet 22.1: The failure workbook

2. Task sheet 22.2: The failure workbook: analysis and review.

3. OHP 22.1.

4. Flipchart.

Description

This activity can be used on training programmes, team-building workshops or for coaching.

Method		Approx time
1	Hand out a copy of Task sheet 22.1: The failure workbook to all participants and ask them to complete it individually. Wherever possible, participants who are going to be in the same group for discussion should complete the Task sheet about an identical initiative or project.	30 mins
2	A lecture may be given at this point on ten generic causes of failure, using OHP 22.1.	10 mins
3	Divide participants into groups with between three and seven members and ask them to complete the task as directed in Task sheet 22.2: The failure workbook: analysis and review.	30 mins
4	Ask groups to present their findings to each other and draw out common themes which should be recorded on a flipchart. The lists can later be typed as a handout from the session.	20 mins

The failure workbook

Identify one significant initiative or large project which you feel was, at least in part, a failure (whenever possible, agree a project in common with the other members of your group). Record a definition of the failed initiative in the box below. Answer the questions strictly in relation to the defined project.

The initiative or project being reviewed is:

Key questions

1. To enable the initiative or project to be successful, were culture changes needed? How well were the culture changes effected? To what extent was the lack of an effective culture change programme a reason for failure?

Needed culture change	What happened	Effects on success/ failure

2. What steps were taken to build the commitment of all involved? How successfully was commitment built? To what extent was lack of commitment a reason for failure?

Who was committed?	Who was not committed?	Effects on success/ failure

3. Were adequate information systems developed that were 'user-friendly'? If not, what were the disadvantages caused by the lack of adequate user-friendly systems? To what extent were information system inadequacies a reason for failure?

These information systems were helpful.	Inadequate information systems had this effect.	In hindsight we needed these information systems.

4. Was impetus maintained? If not, when did impetus start to decline, and why? To what extent was lack of impetus a reason for failure?

These were the stages of the project.	Things went wrong here.

5. Were any shortfalls in skills or know-how quickly addressed? How far did lack of skill or know-how contribute to failure?

We had these skills.	We lacked these skills.	The effect of skill shortfalls was ...

6. Was there a defined plan? How thorough was the plan? Were benchmarks and milestones built in? Did the lack of a defined plan contribute to failure? Why?

Our successes in planning were ...	Our planning inadequacies were ...	With hindsight, we should have planned this way ...

7. How realistic was the plan? What steps were taken to ensure that the plan was tested? Was the lack of realism of the plan a reason for failure?

We were unrealistic in these ways ...	The reasons for lack of realism were ...

8. Was there a willingness to accept superficial analysis or the 'quick fix'?
    If yes, how did this contribute to failure?

When things went wrong we did these things ...	The effects were ...	With hindsight, we should have done these things ...

9. Was there a champion? Did he/she really commit him/herself to the
    success of the initiative or project? Was there anything about the
    behaviour of the champion which contributed to failure?

These behaviours of the champion(s) helped the project.	These behaviours of the champion(s) hindered the project.

10. Was too much taken on at once? Was lack of resources significant? How was this 'lack of focus' allowed to happen? How did management processes contribute to failure?

FACTORS	Led to success	Contributed to failure
a) RESOURCE AVAILABILITY		
b) FOCUS		
c) MANAGEMENT PROCESS		

288

The failure workbook: analysis and review

The members of your group have all completed a review of a failed initiative or project. Your task is to see whether common themes emerge and what could be done differently on another occasion. Discuss each of the ten items on the failure worksheet in order and complete the analysis below.

Issue	This went wrong	Next time we should ...
1. Culture change		
2. Building commitment		
3. User-friendly information systems		
4. Maintaining impetus		
5. Developing skills		

	Issue	This went wrong	Next time we should …
6.	Planning processes		
7.	'Reality testing' plans		
8.	Avoiding the 'quick fix'		
9.	Having skilled champion(s)		
10.	Focusing efforts		

FAILURE – TEN RECIPES FOR DISASTER

1. Don't manage the culture changes needed.

2. Don't build commitment from all involved.

3. Don't develop user-friendly information systems.

4. Don't keep up impetus throughout.

5. Don't develop essential skills.

6. Don't plan thoroughly.

7. Don't test the realism of your plans.

8. Don't do things properly: go for the 'quick fix'.

9. Don't have a skilful champion.

10. Don't limit your efforts; take on too much at once.

Reproduced from *Developing Your People: Easy-to-use activities for improving management skills* by Mike Woodcock and Dave Francis, Gower, Aldershot

23

Theory X – Theory Y: the essence of management style

Objectives

- To explore fundamental approaches to managing people.
- To evaluate personal philosophies of managing people.

Group size

Any number of participants can undertake the activity at the same time.

Time required

Approximately 1 hour.

Materials required

1. Task sheet 23.1: The X–Y scale questionnaire.
2. Task sheet 23.2: The X–Y scale questionnaire: scoring.
3. Task sheet 23.3: The Theory X – Theory Y exercise.
4. OHP 23.1.

Description

To help participants to reflect on their fundamental approach to managing people.

Method		Approx time
1	Invite participants to complete Task sheet 23.1: The X–Y scale questionnaire.	10 mins
2	Give a short lecture on McGregor's Theory X – Theory Y, using OHP 23.1.	10 mins
3	Ask participants to complete Task sheet 23.2: The X–Y scale questionnaire: scoring.	10 mins
4	Divide participants into small groups of three or four to discuss their scores.	10 mins
5	Ask participants to complete Task sheet 23.3: The Theory X – Theory Y exercise.	10 mins
6	Conclude the activity by leading a discussion of the exercise.	10 mins

The X–Y scale questionnaire

Name: _____

Directions

The following are behaviours a manager may use to lead subordinates. Read each item carefully and then put a tick (✓) under the phrase that most accurately describes what you would do.

As a manager I would:	Make a great effort to do this	Tend to do this	Tend to avoid doing this	Make a great effort to avoid this
	(a)	(b)	(c)	(d)
1. Supervise subordinates intensively to draw higher performance from them.	_____	_____	_____	_____
2. Define task objectives for subordinates and convince them of the importance of achieving these.	_____	_____	_____	_____
3. Establish measures to ensure that subordinates are getting the job done.	_____	_____	_____	_____
4. Encourage subordinates to set their own goals.	_____	_____	_____	_____
5. Ensure that subordinates meet the objectives I set for them.	_____	_____	_____	_____
6. Invite subordinates to use my help.	_____	_____	_____	_____
7. Step in as soon as performance measures indicate that a job is slipping.	_____	_____	_____	_____

8. Push people to meet schedules. _____ _____ _____ _____

9. Hold frequent formal and informal meetings to keep in touch with what is going on. _____ _____ _____ _____

10. Allow subordinates to make important decisions themselves if they have relevant experience. _____ _____ _____ _____

The X–Y scale questionnaire: scoring

Directions for scoring

Copy the ticks from Task sheet 23.1 by circling the appropriate letter on the table below. Total the number of circles in each column and multiply by the factor shown to compute your score for each column.

Item number				
1	D	C	B	A
2	D	C	B	A
3	D	C	B	A
4	A	B	C	D
5	A	B	C	D
6	A	B	C	D
7	D	C	B	A
8	D	C	B	A
9	A	B	C	D
10	A	B	C	D
Totals				
	Multiply by 4	Multiply by 3	Multipy by 2	Multipy by 1
Scores				

Total all four scores and place a mark on the scale below to indicate your final score.

297

Reproduced from *Developing Your People: Easy-to-use activities for improving management skills*
by Mike Woodcock and Dave Francis, Gower, Aldershot

Theory X – Theory Y exercise

Directions

There are two 'philosophies' of management which have been characterized as 'Theory X' and 'Theory Y'. Each is based on different sets of assumptions about people.

Read the descriptions below of the two management philosophies. Ask yourself:

- What beliefs do I adopt as a manager?

- What is the likely effect of these beliefs on the people I lead?

- What beliefs would I like to adopt?

- What is preventing me from changing my style of leadership?

Theory X beliefs

1. The average human being has an inherent dislike of work and will avoid it if possible.

2. Because of this human characteristic of dislike for work, most people must be coerced, controlled, directed and threatened with punishment to get them to put forth adequate effort toward the achievement of organizational objectives.

3. The average human being prefers to be directed, wishes to avoid responsibility, has relatively little ambition and wants security above all.

Theory Y beliefs

1. The expenditure of physical and mental effort in work is as natural as play or rest.

2. External control and the threat of punishment are not the only means of bringing about effort toward organizational objectives. People will exercise self-direction and self-control in the service of objectives to which they are committed.

3. Commitment to objectives is a function of the rewards associated with their achievement.

4. The average human being learns under proper conditions not only to accept but also to seek responsibility.

5. The capacity to exercise a high degree of imagination, ingenuity and creativity in the solution of organizational problems is widely, not narrowly, distributed in the population.

6. Under the conditions of modern industrial life, the intellectual potentialities of the average human being are normally only partially utilized.

DOUGLAS McGREGOR's THEORY X – THEORY Y

THEORY X ASSUMPTIONS

- People have an inherent dislike of work.

- External coercion and control are essential.

- Reliance on self-control shows weakness.

- People want to be directed.

- Most people lack creativity.

- Ambition is rare.

- In general, it is foolish to trust people.

THEORY Y ASSUMPTIONS

- Work is a natural activity.

- The threat of punishment reduces motivation.

- Reliance on self-control shows strength.

- People want to set their own direction.

- Most people are creative.

- Ambition is commonplace.

- In general, it is wise to trust people.

Reproduced from *Developing Your People: Easy-to-use activities for improving management skills* by Mike Woodcock and Dave Francis, Gower, Aldershot

24

Leadership review

Objectives

- To enable a leader to review significant aspects of his or her leadership style.

- To provide a checklist of issues which contribute to leadership effectiveness.

- To help in planning personal leadership development.

Group size

Any number of groups with three to seven members.

Time required

Approximately 1 hour.

Materials required

1. Task sheet 24.1: Leadership review.

2. Task sheet 24.2: Leadership review task.

3. OHP 24.1.

Description

This activity was developed for use as a framework for one-to-one counselling but can be adapted for use on training programmes. The activity is particularly useful as an introduction to a session on leadership competencies. The activity can be used by a facilitator or a line manager.

Method		Approx time
1	Introduce the session by referring to the objectives (p.301) and inviting all participants to complete Task sheet 24.1: Leadership review form as directed.	10 mins
2	Divide participants into pairs, and distribute copies of Task sheet 24.2: Leadership review task. This discussion task is completed as directed.	40 mins
3	If desired, conclude the activity by collecting all participants together to share the results of the pair discussions. OHP 24.1, which highlights the 20 leadership factors, can be used as the basis for this final discussion.	10 mins

Leadership review

Instructions

Think about your own leadership style and circle an appropriate number for each item.

1. I am consistent in my behaviour towards subordinates.

    I am inconsistent in my behaviour towards subordinates.

    | 1 | 2 | 3 | 4 | 5 | 6 | 7 |

2. I always keep a degree of social distance from subordinates.

    I often become socially close to my subordinates.

    | 1 | 2 | 3 | 4 | 5 | 6 | 7 |

3. I always help subordinates to learn from experience.

    I usually fail to help subordinates to learn from experience.

    | 1 | 2 | 3 | 4 | 5 | 6 | 7 |

4. I encourage feedback from others on my leadership style.

    I discourage feedback from others on my leadership style.

    | 1 | 2 | 3 | 4 | 5 | 6 | 7 |

5. I encourage questioning from my subordinates.

    I discourage questioning from my subordinates.

    | 1 | 2 | 3 | 4 | 5 | 6 | 7 |

6. I delegate both accountability and responsibility together.

    I do not delegate both accountability and responsibility together.

    | 1 | 2 | 3 | 4 | 5 | 6 | 7 |

7. I have fully analysed the roles that all my subordinates should play.

    I have not fully analysed the roles that all my subordinates should play.

    | 1 | 2 | 3 | 4 | 5 | 6 | 7 |

303

8. I am an effective communicator to my subordinates.

   I do not communicate effectively to my subordinates.

   | 1 | 2 | 3 | 4 | 5 | 6 | 7 |

9. I demonstrate that I fully value the contributions of individuals.

   I do not demonstrate that I fully value the contributions of individuals.

   | 1 | 2 | 3 | 4 | 5 | 6 | 7 |

10. I bring order and structure to meetings.

    I fail to bring order and structure to meetings.

    | 1 | 2 | 3 | 4 | 5 | 6 | 7 |

11. I encourage my subordinates to contribute.

    I do not encourage my subordinates to contribute.

    | 1 | 2 | 3 | 4 | 5 | 6 | 7 |

12. I ensure that objectives are set for my team.

    I fail to ensure that objectives are set for my team.

    | 1 | 2 | 3 | 4 | 5 | 6 | 7 |

13. I give others a sense of optimism.

    I fail to give a sense of optimism to others.

    | 1 | 2 | 3 | 4 | 5 | 6 | 7 |

14. I am willing to take well-defined risks.

    I am unwilling to take well-defined risks.

    | 1 | 2 | 3 | 4 | 5 | 6 | 7 |

15. I am committed to setting high standards.

    I am not committed to setting high standards.

    | 1 | 2 | 3 | 4 | 5 | 6 | 7 |

16. I fight for adequate resources for my subordinates.

    I do not fight for adequate resources for my subordinates.

    | 1 | 2 | 3 | 4 | 5 | 6 | 7 |

17. I have a clear set of values.   I do not have a clear set of values.

| 1 | 2 | 3 | 4 | 5 | 6 | 7 |

18. I am constantly striving for   I am not constantly striving for
     increased efficiency.   increased efficiency.

| 1 | 2 | 3 | 4 | 5 | 6 | 7 |

19. I take great care to develop   I do not take great care to develop
     subordinates' latent talents.   subordinates' latent talents.

| 1 | 2 | 3 | 4 | 5 | 6 | 7 |

20. I persuade others to my point   I fail to persuade others to my
     of view.   point of view.

| 1 | 2 | 3 | 4 | 5 | 6 | 7 |

Leadership review task

Instructions

In discussion with your partner, consider the 20 items on Task sheet 24.1: Leadership review. Identify any areas for improvement and brainstorm what you could do differently in the future. Complete the form on pages 307–8 in the following way:

a) Copy your scores from the leadership review by circling the appropriate number for each item.

b) Examine the high scoring items. Ask 'how important is it that I should consider this further?'

c) Discuss with your partner the issues that you wish to explore further and note any ideas for improvement in the final column. If the time for discussion is limited, ensure that equal time is given to each person.

$$\boxed{\text{T}}$$

Leadership issues (Circle appropriate numbers)	How important is it to explore further? (Score on a 1 to 10 scale)	Ideas for improvement
1. Consistency 1 2 3 4 5 6 7		
2. Social distance 1 2 3 4 5 6 7		
3. Facilitating learning 1 2 3 4 5 6 7		
4. Feedback 1 2 3 4 5 6 7		
5. Questioning 1 2 3 4 5 6 7		
6. Delegating 1 2 3 4 5 6 7		
7. Analysing needs 1 2 3 4 5 6 7		
8. Communication 1 2 3 4 5 6 7		
9. Valuing individuals 1 2 3 4 5 6 7		
10. Structuring meetings 1 2 3 4 5 6 7		

Leadership issues (Circle appropriate numbers)	How important is it to explore further? (Score on a 1 to 10 scale)	Ideas for improvement
11. Encouraging contribution 1 2 3 4 5 6 7		
12. Objective setting 1 2 3 4 5 6 7		
13. Optimism 1 2 3 4 5 6 7		
14. Risk taking 1 2 3 4 5 6 7		
15. Standards 1 2 3 4 5 6 7		
16. Resources 1 2 3 4 5 6 7		
17. Values 1 2 3 4 5 6 7		
18. Efficiency 1 2 3 4 5 6 7		
19. Developing others' talents 1 2 3 4 5 6 7		
20. Persuasion 1 2 3 4 5 6 7		

20 Leadership Review Factors

1. Consistency
2. Social distance
3. Facilitating learning
4. Feedback
5. Questioning
6. Delegating
7. Analysing needs
8. Communication downwards
9. Valuing individuals
10. Structuring meetings
11. Encouraging contribution
12. Objective setting
13. Optimism
14. Risk taking
15. Standards
16. Resources
17. Values
18. Efficiency
19. Developing others' talents
20. Persuasion

25

Innovative leader questionnaire

Objectives

- To explore the characteristics of innovative leaders.
- To provide a format for developing leadership potential.

Group size

Any number of participants can take part at the same time.

Time required

1 hour 15 minutes.

Materials required

1. Task sheet 25.1: Innovative leader questionnaire.
2. Task sheet 25.2: The innovative leader.
3. Task sheet 25.3: Innovative leader worksheet.
4. OHP 25.1.

Description

This activity can be used in any training setting and is also useful for coaching and counselling.

Method		Approx time
1	Introduce the session and invite participants to fill out Task sheet 25.1: Innovative leader questionnaire.	15 mins
2	Give an input on the eight characteristics of innovative leaders, using OHP 25.1.	10 mins
3	Divide participants into pairs or trios to read Task sheet 25.2 and complete the exercise in Task sheet 25.3 as directed.	40 mins
4	Gather learning points and re-emphasize the importance of leaders being innovators.	10 mins

Innovative leader questionnaire

Circle a number for each item as follows:

1   if this statement is totally true about you.

2   if this statement is mainly true about you.

3   if this statement is sometimes true about you.

4   if this statement is rarely true about you.

5   if this statement is never true about you.

The items:

1.	I avoid blaming people for their mistakes.	1	2	3	4	5
2.	I have a stretching vision of how to develop my organization.	1	2	3	4	5
3.	I encourage all ideas.	1	2	3	4	5
4.	I fundamentally question the way we do things.	1	2	3	4	5
5.	I take on a few projects at any one time.	1	2	3	4	5
6.	I explain fully the reasons why we should change.	1	2	3	4	5
7.	I involve people to help think things through.	1	2	3	4	5
8.	I encourage people to improve constantly.	1	2	3	4	5
9.	I do not punish someone for making an unwise suggestion.	1	2	3	4	5
10.	I set demanding goals for improvement.	1	2	3	4	5
11.	I see the potential in embryonic ideas.	1	2	3	4	5
12.	I think radically about how we could improve.	1	2	3	4	5
13.	I prefer to see a few things done properly rather than attempt many projects at once.	1	2	3	4	5
14.	I think through things carefully before taking action.	1	2	3	4	5
15.	I succeed in obtaining resources to get things done.	1	2	3	4	5
16.	I am always improving systems and procedures.	1	2	3	4	5
17.	I encourage people to be creative.	1	2	3	4	5
18.	I am very focused on performance.	1	2	3	4	5

19.	I give people time to develop ideas.	1	2	3	4	5
20.	I take radical ideas from competitors and apply them.	1	2	3	4	5
21.	I see initiatives through to full implementation.	1	2	3	4	5
22.	I can give a full overview of any initiative I undertake.	1	2	3	4	5
23.	I set up temporary teams to get things done.	1	2	3	4	5
24.	I make many improvements and implement them well.	1	2	3	4	5
25.	I do not criticize people who make suggestions.	1	2	3	4	5
26.	I know where I want my organization to be five years' time.	1	2	3	4	5
27.	I can see the potential in an idea.	1	2	3	4	5
28.	I solicit radical opinions on the strengths and weaknesses of my organization.	1	2	3	4	5
29.	I concentrate on achieving a few major changes at any one time.	1	2	3	4	5
30.	I strive to understand things in depth.	1	2	3	4	5
31.	I win support for projects.	1	2	3	4	5
32.	I encourage people to critique their methods and suggest ideas for improvement.	1	2	3	4	5

Reproduced from *Developing Your People: Easy-to-use activities for improving management skills*
by Mike Woodcock and Dave Francis, Gower, Aldershot

Innovative leader questionnaire: scoring and explanation

Directions: Note down your scores for each question on the answer grid below.

1	2	3	4	5	6	7	8
9	10	11	12	13	14	15	16
17	18	19	20	21	22	23	24
25	26	27	28	29	30	31	32
I	II	III	IV	V	VI	VII	VIII

Innovative leader characteristics

The higher your total score in each vertical column, the more you display that particular leadership characteristic. The characteristics are coded as follows:

I   Absence of blame.
II   Stretching visions.
III Support for embryonic ideas.
IV   Questioning orthodoxies.
V   Focus on achievables.
VI   Capacity to develop theories.
VII Exploitation of resources.
VIII Continuous improvement ethic.

315

Reproduced from *Developing Your People: Easy-to-use activities for improving management skills* by Mike Woodcock and Dave Francis, Gower, Aldershot

The innovative leader

Directions

Read the explanation of the eight innovative leadership characteristics and then discuss your own scores with one or two others.

Innovative leader characteristics

I ABSENCE OF BLAME

Blame (demonstrated through criticism or lack of respect) has the effect of limiting an individual's willingness to be innovative. Few are willing to risk going outside conventional thinking if there is a possibility that they will be pilloried for their creativity or radicalness. The innovative leader creates, through example, an atmosphere where it is acceptable to be bold and different. Unconventional ideas are heard and respected, even if they are not implemented.

II STRETCHING VISIONS

One of the key roles of the leader is to encapsulate and communicate a vision of how things could and should be. The articulation of a vision invariably clarifies the gap between the 'now' situation and the 'desired' situation. This 'gap', once understood, is a spur to innovation. People begin to consider how the gap can be filled and innovative suggestions emerge. From time to time the innovative leader needs to redefine the vision so that it is relevant and has the right degree of stretch.

III SUPPORT FOR EMBRYONIC IDEAS

Creativity is an untidy process. Ideas are frequently flawed or under-developed. The innovative leader has the wisdom to see the potential in latent ideas and give them nourishment. Just as a gardener cares for young plants, so the innovative leader will support suggestions and allow them to grow, adding both psychological and practical support.

IV QUESTIONING ORTHODOXIES

Every organization develops orthodoxies – formulas for success. These become enshrined in the culture and systems of the firm and become unquestioned givens. Changing technologies and environmental forces can

Reproduced from *Developing Your People: Easy-to-use activities for improving management skills* by Mike Woodcock and Dave Francis, Gower, Aldershot

render organizational orthodoxies irrelevant but the habit patterns are so strong that they are not challenged. The innovative leader is prepared to 'question the givens' and explore fundamentally different ways of doing things. This requires a mental agility and openness that must be tempered by prudence – it is easy to sweep away valued customs and practices in an over-eager pursuit of change.

V   FOCUS ON ACHIEVABLES

Not everything can be achieved at once. If efforts are dissipated in too many initiatives at one time, then innovations are not implemented – as the necessary focus of effort is absent. It is better to concentrate on a few objectives and carry them through to implementation rather than fritter away energy on a larger number of desirable but unresourced initiatives. One of the important skills for the innovative leader is selecting a narrow range of initiatives and then ensuring that these are fully driven through.

VI   CAPACITY TO DEVELOP THEORIES

The word 'theory' is often used to condemn an idea as being impractical. In fact, theories are immensely practical and innovative leaders develop theories to guide their decision making. Assume that a retail manager wants to introduce an innovative scheme for staffing the store flexibly. She/he needs a theory which combines forecasting customer loading and motivating the types of staff needed. Once a theory is available, then plans follow naturally.

VII   EXPLOITATION OF RESOURCES

Innovation often requires a temporary organization to get things done. This may require specific skills equipment, intellectual capital, funds and so on. Innovative managers have the capacity to assess resource requirements and make these available. This is more difficult than it sounds. Often technical capabilities have to be integrated with routine operations and new technologies may need to be mastered. The innovative leader is a specialist in finding, aligning, exploiting and integrating a wide range of potential resources.

VIII   CONTINUOUS IMPROVEMENT ETHIC

Since almost any situation can be improved, the innovative leader needs to adopt an attitude of 'creative dissatisfaction'. This is not any easy stance to take as it can be viewed as demeaning past efforts. However, although past achievement ought to be honoured, the innovative leader should adopt the attitude that incremental improvements must flow like a river. Nothing can be accepted unconditionally. Even small innovations, when amassed, produce significant changes and improvements.

Innovative leader worksheet

Meet with one or two others. Share the results of your questionnaire and answer these questions:

1. What are my innovation strengths?

INNOVATION STRENGTHS	WHERE SHOWN?

2. What are my innovation weaknesses?

INNOVATION WEAKNESSES	EFFECT ON OTHERS

318

3. These are the actions I could take to strengthen innovation in my leadership style:

ACTIONS I COULD TAKE	OPPORTUNITIES	WAYS I WOULD JUDGE 'SUCCESS'

INNOVATIVE LEADERS ...

I DON'T BLAME

II HAVE A STRETCHING VISION

III SUPPORT EMBRYONIC IDEAS

IV QUESTION ORTHODOXIES

V FOCUS ON ACHIEVABLES

VI DEVELOP USEFUL THEORIES

VII EXPLOIT RESOURCES

VIII CONTINUOUSLY IMPROVE
EVERYTHING

26

Cozibears: a case study in organizational design

Objectives

- To introduce new models of constituting organizations.

- To develop a critical awareness of the strengths and weaknesses of different methods of constructing organizations.

Group size

1. It is appropriate for managers who have responsibility for organizational design, and for students of organization and management.

2. Any number of participants can take part at the same time.

Time required

1 hour.

Materials required

1. Handout 26.1: The Cozibears case study.

2. Task sheet 26.1: Your task.

3. OHPs 26.1–26.4.

Description

This activity introduces four 'new' models of organization.

Method		Approx time
1	Introduce the case study and form groups with three to five members.	5 mins
2	Ask participants to read Handout 26.1: The Cozibears case study and take 40 minutes to discuss the issues as directed in Task sheet 26.1. Inform the participants that they can, if they wish, have access to OHPs of the four organizational types (OHPs 26.1–26.4) which are discussed in the text. These may be used for presentations.	40 mins
3	Invite groups to share their analysis and recommendations.	15 mins

The Cozibears case study

Cozibears (Cozi for short) is a supplier of traditional stuffed animals specializing, as their name suggests, in many and varied kinds of bear. Obviously their target market is parents and children but, sometimes, there are secondary customers. For example, a large oil company recently invited Cozibears to tender to supply 100 000 chauffeur bears as part of a promotional offer. (However, Cozi lost the order to a Vietnamese bear manufacturer who was able to offer lower prices.)

The Cozibears organization has six main activities. These are:

- Designing new bears.

- Prototyping new designs and variations of existing models.

- Marketing a wide range of bears.

- Selling to key accounts, independent shops and by mail order.

- Manufacturing bears in factories in Birmingham, UK and Hamilton, Ontario.

- Distributing stocks of bears to retailers.

Each of these activities takes place in the UK or Canada, with the exception of Snowy Christmas Bears, which are made by a sub-contractor in Zaire in a United Nations-sponsored factory.

Unfortunately, the company is performing badly: costs are rising and increasingly aggressive competition is shrinking margins. Profits are zero and the bank manager is anxious. Despite the company's financial problems the potential market is huge, with new sales leads arriving by fax and post every week. However, when these opportunities are evaluated, Cozibears' profit is either zero or minuscule – other competitors in low-cost economies can provide bears more cheaply.

In an attempt to find a new strategy, the directors of Cozi decided to call in a leading consultant, Professor C.K. Handberg, to run a half-day seminar for the top management group. This, they hoped, would stimulate a radical review so that the business could be repositioned and return to profit. As Tom Ollins, Chief Executive, said, 'We want Cozi to be a name to play with for future generations'. Professor Handberg affirmed that Cozi was a powerful brand name and that a wide range of market opportunities existed. However he said, with a dramatic flurry of arms, that the organization was at a cross-roads and the directors had to make a choice about how to develop their business. He said there were four principal options:

1. Remain a functionally integrated firm and take cost out of all activities

which do not add marketing advantages.

2. Become a 'virtual organization' – combining with others opportunistically to seize market possibilities.

3. Become a 'clover-leaf organization', buying in all but core, value-adding services.

4. Become a 'boundaryless organization' and break down traditional barriers to act faster and more intelligently.

Tom Ollins felt pleased he was up to date with his reading on management and said, 'Just let me think this through with you, Professor. I would like to relate these four options to Cozi. I think you are saying this:

'First, we could streamline Cozi's operations and review all of our activities to see where we could take cost out of the business without sacrificing quality, flexibility, and so on. This might mean manufacturing in Vietnam, not selling to small independent stores, and so on.

'Second, we could do only those things which we are really good at (which for us is designing bears and marketing to a traditional trade) and close our manufacturing, distribution and, maybe, even our sales divisions. We would team, as needed, with independent firms which have the other capabilities we need. This would be on a flexible basis and enable us to do just that in which we excel. We could deal with changing seasonal and marketing requirements with very low costs (providing we can find good partners!).

'Third, we could shrink to a core of activities and buy in all the other services that we need. For example, we could give work to specialist manufacturers in low-wage countries, enter into a contract with a distribution firm and so on. This option, unlike number two, puts us in charge of our strategy and we could change partners if we find the suppliers do not meet our cost or performance targets.

'Last, we could keep the firm more or less as it is but change our attitudes to working together. It is true that we have a silo mentality and departments work as independent cells. If we could break these insular attitudes down and get information flowing then we would develop new products very quickly and seize market opportunities, because we would work together more effectively and our speed of innovation should give us a competitive edge.'

The Professor smiled and said, 'You have got it, but to make it really clear let me draw a diagram.' With that he went to the flipchart and drew the four options shown on pages 325–6.

The four options

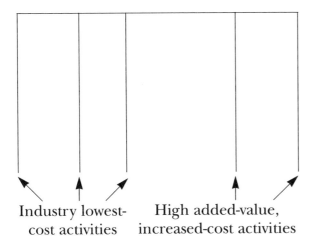

Option 1
Competitive functional organization

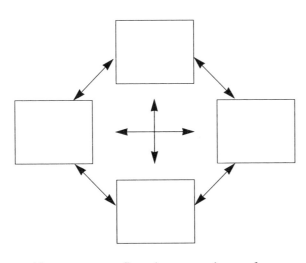

Option 2
Virtual organization

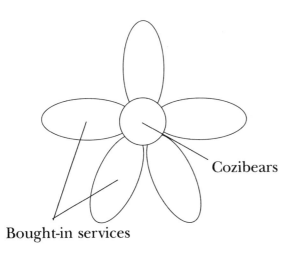

Option 3
Clover-leaf organization

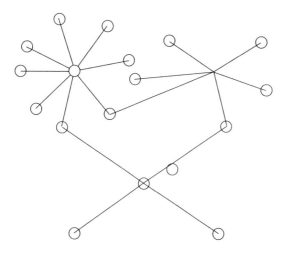

Option 4
Boundaryless organization

No walls, networking everywhere.

At that point the Professor said, 'We all understand the basic concept but there are no right answers. We all know that Cozi needs to change and I am going to divide you into groups to discuss these four options, develop a list of strengths and weaknesses for each and make a recommendation as to which you feel would be most likely to remedy Cozibears' strategic weaknesses.'

Your task

Assume that you are a member of Cozibears' management team. Evaluate the four organizational design options that the Professor described against Cozibears' business problems. Which would you recommend?

1. COMPETITIVE FUNCTIONAL ORGANIZATION

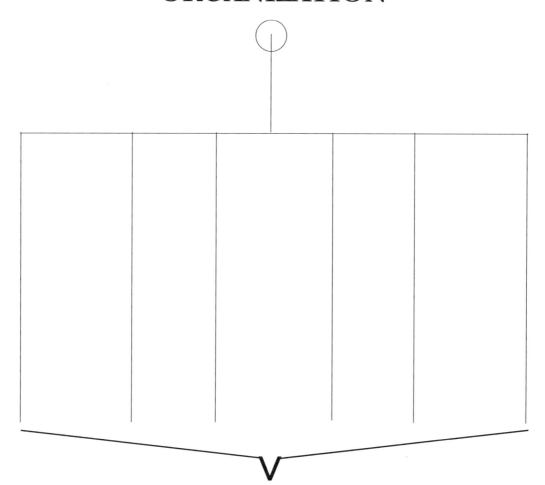

INDUSTRY LOWEST-COST AND HIGH-VALUE, HIGH-COST ACTIVITIES

2. VIRTUAL ORGANIZATION

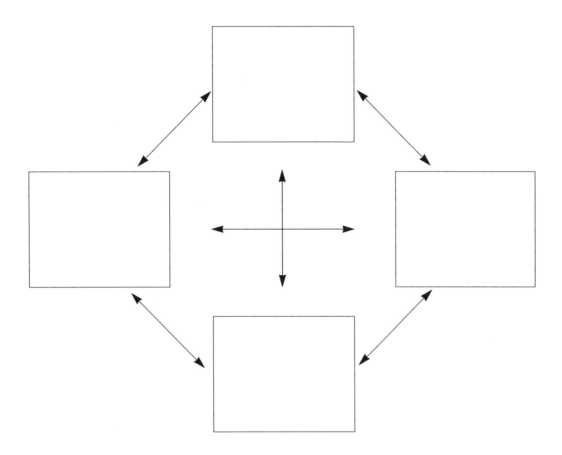

ALWAYS RE-CONFIGURING TO SUIT MARKETS

3. CLOVER-LEAF ORGANIZATION

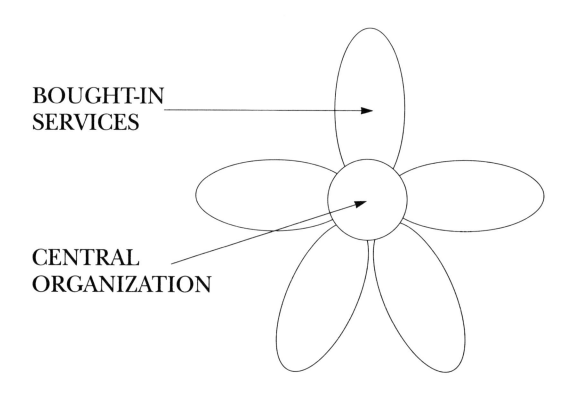

BOUGHT-IN
SERVICES

CENTRAL
ORGANIZATION

4. BOUNDARYLESS ORGANIZATION

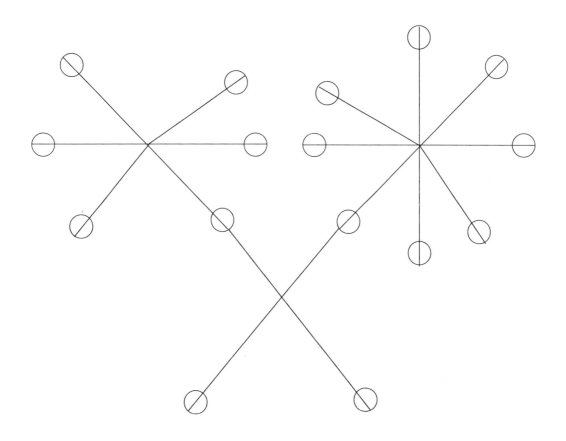

NO WALLS, NETWORKING EVERYWHERE

331

27

Situational management

Objectives

- To develop a typology of management skills.
- To relate individual management skills to organizational contexts.
- To explore the competencies required by managers in different types of organizations.

Group size

Any number of participants can take part in the activity at the same time.

Time required

1 hour 15 minutes.

Materials required

1. Task sheet 27.1: Situational management questionnaire.
2. Task sheet 27.2: Scoring and explanation sheet.
3. Task sheet 27.3: Assignment sheet.
4. OHPs 27.1–27.6.

Description

This activity is designed for use in management training courses but can also be used for managerial counselling and coaching. The Situational management questionnaire is based on a model developed by Henry Mintzberg and published in *The Structuring of Organizations: A Synthesis of Research* (Prentice Hall, Englewood Cliffs, NJ, 1979).

Method		Approx time
1	Introduce the activity and ask participants to complete Task sheet 27.1: Situational management questionnaire as directed.	15 mins
2	Give a lecture on the five organizational configurations used as a model for this questionnaire, using OHPs 27.1 to 27.6. This can be derived from Chapter 6 of *Unblocking Organizational Communication* by Dave Francis (Gower, Aldershot, 1987) or Henry Mintzberg's book, previously noted.	15 mins
3	Form participants into pairs or trios and give out Task sheet 27.2: Scoring and explanation sheet. Give out Task sheet 27.3: Assignment sheet and ask for it to be completed as directed.	30 mins for pairs 45 mins for trios

Situational management questionnaire

Reflect on the items below in relation to your current job and assign points as appropriate, noting them in the relevant box.

The statement is generally true   3 points
The statement is partly true   1 point
The statement is generally untrue   0 points

1. I personally control every aspect of what goes on in my part of the organization.

2. I work to a plan and eliminate 'surprises'.

3. I manage people who have highly developed professional skills.

4. I give my subordinates a 'free rein' within well-defined objectives.

5. I create a context in which experts can be creative.

6. I have information systems which allow me to make all the important decisions in my part of the organization.

7. I strive to standardize every activity.

8. I convey principles and policies, but leave a great deal of discretion to highly trained staff.

9. I recruit excellent staff and leave them to handle all operational issues.

10. I am constantly reorganizing the people within my area of responsibility.

11. I make all the key decisions in my part of the organization.

12. I insist on rigid job descriptions for all positions.

13. I frequently organize learning events so that the staff can keep up to date.

14. I feel too remote to make operational decisions, so I delegate substantial responsibility within defined performance objectives.

15. I frequently call meetings so that we can decide together what is the best thing to do next.

335

16. If I decide to make a change, I don't ask anyone but issue the appropriate instructions.

17. I try to make the organization run like a well-oiled machine.

18. I work with the professionals in my part of the organization to achieve a consensus on priorities.

19. I only review performance indicators and avoid getting involved in details.

20. I spend a great deal of time building effective teams to handle new projects.

21. I don't really share power; everyone knows that I am the boss.

22. I insist on strict adherence to rules and regulations.

23. I manage by persuasion, almost never giving orders.

24. I make decisions on broad objectives and leave detailed work to my subordinates.

25. I am a strong project manager.

26. I keep communication lines very short.

27. Even though many employees have repetitive tasks, I seek to make work more interesting.

28. I see my primary task as enabling trained professionals to use their skills.

29. I specify what has to be achieved, not how to do it.

30. I fight to keep my organization flexible and adaptable.

31. If I am away from work, important things do not get done.

32. I ensure that there is a system which defines what actions should be performed whatever occurs.

33. I chair meetings and persuade my staff in order to get things done within my area of responsibility.

34. I only interfere when performance is unacceptable.

35. I am constantly reviewing whether we need to reorganize.

36. I hand-pick all new staff.

37. I measure performance against predetermined standards.

38. I shape my staff's attitudes rather than issue directives.

39. I act in the role of management consultant to those who work for me.

40. I create excitement, not rules and regulations.

41. I personally make all the decisions about strategy in my part of the organization.

42. I insist that performance on every activity is measured against objective criteria.

43. I listen to my subordinates and try to provide them with all the resources that they need.

44. I select subordinates and leave them to 'run their own show'.

45. I convey the results I want achieved, but often do not know how to get there myself.

46. I control the organization by directly supervising all staff.

47. I ensure that each member of staff has a precise job description.

48. I look upon the people who report to me as colleagues – not subordinates.

49. I ensure that there are strong and independent teams in each division or unit of my organization.

50. I encourage creativity, not obedience.

Task sheet 27.2 (page 1 of 6)

Scoring and explanation sheet

Copy your scores on to the answer grid below and read the explanation on the following pages.

1		2		3		4		5	
6		7		8		9		10	
11		12		13		14		15	
16		17		18		19		20	
21		22		23		24		25	
26		27		28		29		30	
31		32		33		34		35	
36		37		38		39		40	
41		42		43		44		45	
46		47		48		49		50	
Totals I		II		III		IV		V	

Explanation

I. SIMPLE STRUCTURE

If you score high in section I, you are a manager who works well in a simple structure.

Small organizations (or larger organizations in crisis) thrive under clear 'hands-on' leadership by a boss. Complexity, excess staff, over-elaborate systems and formality are enemies. The organization must be kept simple

338

Reproduced from *Developing Your People: Easy-to-use activities for improving management skills*
by Mike Woodcock and Dave Francis, Gower, Aldershot

and flexible, with the boss in control. He or she makes decisions, seizes opportunities, and aggressively confronts the world. The simple structure hinges on the health and drive of one person. Expansion is limited, since the lack of formal organization prevents the management of large tasks.

The key competency factors required to manage an effective simple structure are:

1. An excellent boss.

2. Information systems which keep the boss constantly in touch.

3. Strong specialist managers.

4. Much flexibility.

5. Central control and co-ordination.

6. Rapid communication.

7. The 'small is beautiful' philosophy.

8. Hand-picked staff.

9. Simple but effective financial control.

10. Very clear strategic focus.

II. MECHANISTIC ORGANIZATION

If you score high in section II, you are a manager who works well in a mechanistic organization.

Some organizations, such as airlines or post offices, have routine tasks to perform predictably time and time again. In order to be efficient, the organization develops like a machine. Jobs become highly specialized and training is essential. There are many rules and regulations. Communication and decision making are formalized, elaborate and intricate. Specialized departments are led by managers who are expert in their particular discipline. Specialists such as work study analysts, accountants, quality controllers and planners proliferate: without them, the organization would collapse into chaos. Managers are 'obsessed' with control, trying to measure all variables and eliminate uncertainty.

Although the mechanistic type of organization is technically efficient, there are latent conflicts which threaten productivity. People at the lower end of the organization find the controls and regulations dehumanizing. Sometimes it is virtually impossible to introduce a humanistic environment into a system that is essentially a machine. Such organizations are hierarchical and predictable. Discipline, standard setting and effective human resource management are essential. The organization has built-in inertia and has to be constantly reviewed.

The key competency factors required to manage an effective machine

339

structure are:

1. A stable environment.

2. Highly developed co-ordination systems.

3. Competent technical specialists.

4. An efficient bureaucracy.

5. A disciplined workforce.

6. Antidotes to dehumanizing work.

7. Clarity about the tasks to be done.

8. Managers who demand performance.

9. Regular assessments on every activity.

10. Reward for performance.

III. PROFESSIONAL ORGANIZATION

If you score high in section III, you are a manager who works well in a professional organization.

Some organizations require highly trained individuals to meet complex and unpredictable requirements from the customer. This form of organization is dependent on the competency of highly educated and skilled workers who must be trusted to do the job 'professionally'. The organization provides an environment which sets basic standards and then enables the professionals to get on with their work within this structure.

Careers in professional organizations begin with a comparatively large amount of training and education. Professional skills and attitudes take years to acquire and accumulate and must then be regularly updated. Professionals have to learn to avoid both simplistic rule making and abdication from responsibility. Administrators develop a steering and co-ordinating role. Power is largely decentralized and the overall leadership style is persuasive rather than autocratic. The professional organization often experiences political scheming. Influence, rather than rational argument, can rule the day. Innovation, which requires the co-operation of colleagues, is notoriously difficult to orchestrate. In fact, creative thinking often fails to flourish in such organizations, since individuals prefer to work along time-proven lines. Change can only taken place with the willing co-operation of many independent people, and it often proceeds painfully slowly. However, in spite of all the disadvantages, organizations that require people to perform a wide variety of unpredictable and complex tasks have no option but to place control in the hands of the professionals. Nothing else had been proven to work.

The key competency factors required to manage an effective professional

T

structure are:

1. Highly trained workers.

2. Clear organizational values.

3. Much on-going training.

4. A consensus on priorities.

5. Persuasive managers.

6. Efficient support staff.

7. Dynamic committee structure.

8. Strong positive group norms.

9. Effective distributed leadership.

10. Effective methods for recognizing and penalizing low performance.

IV. *DIVISIONALIZED ORGANIZATION*

If you score high in section IV, you are a manager who works well in a divisionalized organization.

Most large organizations have learned that over-centralization is clumsy, so they evolve into specialized divisions streamlined for specific markets. The divisions are semi-independent units devoted to a limited range of products and are co-ordinated by a headquarters that directs the overall strategy.

In divisionalized organizations, decision making is pushed downward and independent divisions are formed, each having a full complement of analysts and support staff. This is costly in overheads, but it allows units to be independently accountable.

Each unit or division develops its own goals, which it negotiates with headquarters. Quantitative measures are required; without them, control cannot be exercised. Headquarters allows a lot of freedom but carefully monitors results. Much day-to-day authority is given to middle managers whose skills are critical.

A sympathetic use of both carrot and stick best describes the relationship between headquarters and division. Headquarters retains control over criteria for measuring results, allocation of major financial resources, control systems, appointment of key personnel, basic research, and formulation of key policies. The units focus their attention on the markets they know, and attempt to exploit them. The division tries to act like a horse pounding toward the finishing line.

The key competency factors required to manage an effective divisionalized structure are:

1. A fully developed performance control system.

341

2.   Excellent divisional general managers.

3.   Defined strategies for each of the divisions.

4.   Strong focus on defined markets.

5.   Competent portfolio management at headquarters level.

6.   Stretching performance targets.

7.   Relative freedom from interference from the top (in good times!).

8.   Consultancy services from headquarters.

9.   Incisive performance evaluations from headquarters.

10.   Strong functional teams in each of the divisions.

V.   ADHOCRACY

If you score high in section V, you are a manager who works well in an adhocracy.

The previous four kinds of organization are best suited to managing existing and largely predictable situations. When something big and dramatically new has to be done then a 'large but organic' organization is best. If you need to build a new-generation computer or develop a strategy for the refurbishment of a run-down city then the rather formal options that we've already discussed are inappropriate; a flexible team approach is necessary.

Innovation requires people to break away from established patterns; standardization or formalization stifles creativity and inhibits experiment. This needs an organization that is anti-bureaucratic and co-ordinated by frequent meetings and *ad hoc* arrangements. Clear job demarcations, invariable routines and bureaucratic disciplines aren't helpful. All manner of communication techniques must be used to co-ordinate work, and change is often needed. A good example of an organic organization is NASA. In the first eight years of its life, this organization changed its structure 17 times. And it did land men on the moon on schedule.

Large organic organizations can grow complex and untidy – often using complex managerial arrangements – yet this is essential to their innovative vitality. Employees, especially managers, develop skills in handling bewildering and divergent situations. They become expert co-ordinators and resource allocators. Power is held by those who have the expertise rather than by formal bosses. Top management has the key role of accumulating resources and reassigning specialists to meet the needs of the moment. Strategy is reviewed many times as new facts emerge, and long-term planning may actually impede achievement since only the originators of ideas know what's needed to get the tasks done. Top managers spend much time identifying strategic options and clarifying broad objectives. They strive to make choices on the basis of highly complex arguments and, although they try to control, they often find that they can only decide after the event whether an investment has been worthwhile.

The key competency factors required to manage an effect large organic structure are:

1. Real experts in key jobs.

2. Willingness to change constantly.

3. Constant reviews of progress.

4. Much team building.

5. Project management skills.

6. Fight against bureaucratic formalization.

7. Fight against individuals seeking their own self-interest.

8. Technologically knowledgeable managers.

9. Emphasis on the outputs required.

10. Efficient links with other organizations.

Task sheet 27.3 (page 1 of 1)

Assignment sheet

Meet with one or two others to discuss the results of the questionnaire. Divide the time available equally, and for each participant answer the following questions:

1. What are your strengths as a manager?

2. In what situations are these strengths appropriate?

3. What management strengths are required by your current job?

4. What could be done to improve your management skills in your current job?

What could be done?	How could this be done?

1. FIVE ORGANIZATIONAL TYPES

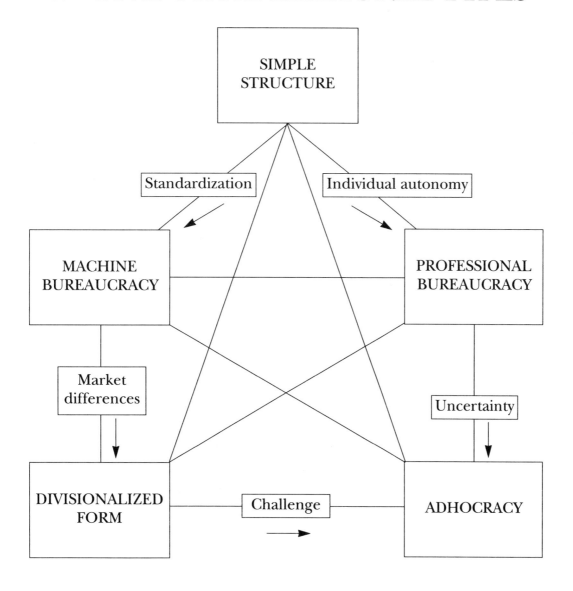

345

Reproduced from *Developing Your People: Easy-to-use activities for improving management skills*
by Mike Woodcock and Dave Francis, Gower, Aldershot

2. Simple structure

Characteristics

1. An excellent boss with all-round competencies.

2. Information systems which keep the boss in touch all the time.

3. Strong subordinates – each expert in their own area.

4. Seeing and taking advantage of opportunities.

5. Central control and co-ordination.

6. Rapid communication.

7. Using 'smallness' as a virtue.

8. Hand-picked, able and loyal staff.

9. Simple but effective financial control.

10. Very clear strategic focus.

3.   Machine form

Characteristics

1.   Ability to maintain a stable environment.

2.   Highly developed co-ordination systems between departments.

3.   Competent technical specialists in all functional areas.

4.   Efficient formal systems which structure jobs.

5.   A disciplined workforce.

6.   Reduction of 'dehumanizing' work.

7.   Great clarity about the tasks to be done.

8.   Managers demand performance from employees.

9.   Regular assessments of every activity.

10.   Reward for performance.

4. Professional form

Characteristics

1. Highly trained workers.

2. Clear organizational values.

3. Much on-going training.

4. A deep consensus on priorities.

5. Persuasive managers who pull together specialists.

6. Efficient support staff to back up professionals.

7. Positive committees to make decisions.

8. Strong positive group norms which encourage high performance through peer pressure.

9. Competent leadership from specialists.

10. Effective methods for recognizing and dealing with low performance.

5. Diversified form

Characteristics

1. Competent portfolio management at HQ level (being in the 'right' businesses).

2. HQ gives substantial freedom to divisions.

3. Incisive performance evaluations of divisions from HQ.

4. Strategic consultancy services from HQ.

5. Excellent divisional general managers.

6. Strong functional teams in each of the divisions.

7. A fully developed performance control system.

8. Well-defined strategies for each of the divisions.

9. Strong focus on defined markets.

10. Performance targets that really challenge the divisions.

6. Adhocracy

Characteristics

1. Real experts in key jobs.

2. Willing and able to change constantly.

3. Constant reviews of progress.

4. Much team building.

5. Project management skills.

6. Fight against bureaucratic formalization.

7. Fight against individuals seeking their own self-interest.

8. Being efficient and informal.

9. Emphasis on the outputs required.

10. Capacity to combine disciplines to solve problems.

Reproduced from *Developing Your People: Easy-to-use activities for improving management skills*
by Mike Woodcock and Dave Francis, Gower, Aldershot

28

Team communication: the whisper chain*

Objectives

- To explore communication difficulties with a dispersed team.
- To develop team communication skills.

Group size

This is a team exercise for groups with four members. Observers can be allocated to teams. As many groups as desired can participate at the same time.

Time required

Approximately 1 hour.

Materials required

1. Task sheet 28.1: Activity brief: team communication.

2. Task sheet 28.2: Team connunication review.

3. 3 index card boxes

4. 100 index cards.

* The authors wish to thank Helene Francis for this activity.

5. One pen.

Description

To explore the things that can go wrong in verbal communication.

Method		Approx time

1	*Preparation:*
	Prepare the materials required to carry out the instructions in this task as follows:
	
	● Place three index card boxes on a table; label the boxes A, B and C.
	
	● Place 12 index cards in box A. A different name should be written on each card (first name and family name, for example Anita Lang; John Bird and so on); the cards should be 'filed' in the box in a random order. Each card should be given a different number from 1–12 at random. Numbers should be written on the top right-hand corner of the cards.
	
	● Place about 20 index cards in box B; a different name should be written on each card (first name and family name). The cards should be filed in the box in alphabetical order. The following names must be used on eight of the cards:
	
	  1. Brenda Young 2. Billy Ling
	  3. Phyllis Leung 4. K. C. Leung
	  5. Tony Leung 6. Richard Goldsmidt
	  7. Peter Jackson 8. Janet Jackson
	
	● Place about 20 index cards in box C. A different name should be written on each card (first name and family name). The cards should be filed in the box in alphabetical order.
		15 mins

Method		Approx time
	• Place a pile of blank index cards and a pen on the table at the side of the boxes. **Note:** The index cards will need to be re-arranged after each group has completed the exercise; alternatively you may wish to have several identical sets of the boxes available. *Procedure*	
2	Begin the activity by gathering one member from each of the groups in the main training room. All other course participants should go to the appropriate location indicated in the Activity brief. **Note:** the purpose of this exercise is to explore how a complex message can be communicated orally. For this reason participants may not see the Activity brief. • Put the contents of box A in numerical order. • Remove Young; Ling; Leung; Goldsmidt and Jackson from box B and file them in alphabetical order in box C. • Write the names James Goldstone, Sara Lau and Patrick O'Keefe on separate index cards; file them in alphabetical order in box B. **Note:** The names on the index cards can be changed to reflect the culture in which the activity is conducted.	5 mins
3	Read out the message – and the instructions and rules as indicated in the Activity brief – to the assembled group members. The group members may not have sight of the brief although they may make notes. The facilitator should read out the brief as many times as is requested.	2–5 mins

	Method	Approx time
4	Read out the message again slowly and answer any questions of clarification but do not engage in discussion about the task and the meaning of the instructions. Group members must not be shown the materials for carrying out the instructions.	5 mins
5	Ask the group members if anyone would like to hear the message again and explain that as soon as they are ready (that is, they can remember the message to their satisfaction) team members can leave and begin passing on the message to the next person in line in their whisper chain. Continue re-reading the message until everyone has left.	5 mins
6	When the last person has left the room, place the table containing all the materials in the middle of the room.	
7	Note the finish time for each of the groups and the number of errors made in carrying out the instructions. Add one minute to the time taken for every error made by a group in carrying out the instructions. Post the results during the break.	
8	When all groups have completed the task (or abandoned it!), ask them to complete a short review using Task sheet 28.2: Team communication review.	10 mins

Activity brief: team communication

Whisper chain

The purpose of this activity is to demonstrate the importance of giving and receiving communication clearly.

You will be assigned to work in a small group to complete the Whisper chain task, and your group will be in competition with other groups.

Your group's task is to pass from one member to another an oral message which conveys a set of instructions. All members of the group must participate. The last person in your group to receive the message must carry out the instructions it contains.

Select the order in which you will pass on the message in your group. The group member who goes first will receive the message orally from the trainer, at the same time as one member of the other group(s). The remaining group members should go to the following locations:

2nd person in the chain: approximately 25 metres from main training room.

3rd person in the chain: approximately 15 metres from 2nd person in chain.

4th (last) person in chain: approximately 15 metres from 3rd person in chain.

When the last person in the chain has received the message, they should return to the main training room where they will be asked to carry out the instructions contained in the message. All group members are allowed into the room to watch the carrying out of instructions; however they must remain silent during this stage of the activity.

Remember!

There is no time limit for this activity, but groups will be in competition. The winning group will be the one which completes the task correctly in the shortest time.

Rules for giving and receiving the message

● The message can be repeated as many times as team members wish.

● As soon as the receiver is satisfied that he/she can remember the message, he/she can go to the next person in the chain.

Reproduced from *Developing Your People: Easy-to-use activities for improving management skills* by Mike Woodcock and Dave Francis, Gower, Aldershot

- When senders have passed on the message, they must return at once directly to the training room; they must not communicate with any other team member(s) about the content of the message.

- The receiver can ask the sender questions for clarification.

- Group members may use any oral techniques they wish to help them remember the message.

- No part of the message may be communicated in a written form of any kind.

Reproduced from *Developing Your People: Easy-to-use activities for improving management skills* by Mike Woodcock and Dave Francis, Gower, Aldershot

Team communication review

Answer the following questions as a group.

1.

What helped your group?	What hindered your group?

2. If you were to do the exercise again, what would you do differently?

We would do these things differently ...	For these reasons ...

29

Team feedback

Objectives

- To clarify roles in teams and between interdependent people.

- To provide a format for giving task-oriented feedback between team members.

- To assist team members to manage interdependence and gain advantages of synergy.

Group size

Unlimited (but the participants must have interdependent jobs).

Time required

2 hours.

Materials required

(Sufficient copies for each team member to send one to every other member of the team.)

1. Task sheet 29.1: Team feedback message sheet.

2. Task sheet 29.2: Team feedback worksheet.

3. OHP 29.1.

Description

To clarify participants' roles in relation to others.

	Method	Approx time
1	Introduce the session by describing the stages of the activity using OHP 29.1. Distribute a set of Task sheet 29.1: Team feedback message sheet (a set equals the total number of team members minus one) to each participant. The leader asks each member to fill out a message sheet as instructed for every other member of the team.	20 mins
2	Participants wait until all messages have been written and then deliver them to the recipients.	5 mins
3	Each person privately reads the messages received.	10 mins
4	Ask each team member, in turn, to read out the messages received and seek maximum clarity and understanding of the messages by openly discussing them. Encourage members to make specific feedback statements to the recipient, with examples of behaviour. The recipient should ask for clarification and should not be defensive: the purpose is to understand the perceptions of other team members.	60 mins
5	After each discussion, team members reflect on what they will do differently and then complete Task sheet 29.2: Team feedback worksheet.	10 mins
6	Team members share their resolutions to behave differently by reading out (elaborating if necessary) the completed Team feedback worksheet.	15 mins

Team feedback message sheet

MESSAGE FROM: TO:

It would help me in my job if you would...

Do the following more or better:
Do the following less, or stop doing them:
Continue doing the following:
Start doing these additional things:

Team feedback worksheet

Directions

Following the feedback you have received, decide what you will do differently in the future. Record these below:

In future I will do the following more or better:

In future I will do the following less or stop doing them:

I will continue to do these:

In future I will do these new things:

TEAM FEEDBACK

WHAT TO DO...

1. Complete a message sheet for each other team member.

2. When completed, exchange message sheets and consider the feedback.

3. Take turns to read out the feedback you received and ask for clarification.

4. Decide what (if anything) you will do differently in future.

5. Announce your decisions to the team. Ask for support if necessary.

30

Intergroup efficiency

Objectives

- To clarify the benefits of setting objectives for inter-team achievement.
- To develop skills in setting inter-team objectives.
- To explore the management of collaboration between teams.

Group size

At least 12 people will be needed to undertake the exercise successfully.

Time required

1 hour 20 minutes.

Materials required

1. Task sheet 30.1: Task one.
2. Task sheets 30.2–30.5: Task two: Group A, B, C, D.

Description

This exercise was devised for use in a training environment and can be used to precede a lecture on objective setting.[1]

Method		Approx time
1	Form four groups with a minimum of three people in each group. Inform each group that it is about to undertake two experiments in intergroup co-operation but give no further explanation.	5 mins
2	Give each group a copy of Task sheet 30.1: Task one and ask them to complete it in 30 minutes.	30 mins
3	Following the preparation period bring all four groups together to give their presentation. Stop the presentation after 5 minutes and conduct a brief review of the quality of the intergroup work.	10 mins
4	Divide the group into the same four sub-groups and asked them to undertake Task two. This time give each group a separate brief (Task sheets 30.2–5, labelled A, B, C and D).	20 mins
5	Ask all four groups to come together and give their presentation. Stop the presentation after 5 minutes and conduct a review of the quality of the intergroup work. Particular attention should be paid to the benefits of the increased clarity of objectives in the second task. These questions may help the facilitator review the task: • Where were you more rushed for time – the first or second task? • Which of the two presentations had the better content? • How was communication between the groups affected by the increased clarity of objectives in the second task? • Were there any disadvantages to the task clarify in the second task? • How can you use the skills of shared objective setting in your own jobs?	15 mins

1. For more information on goal setting see Mike Woodcock and Dave Francis, *The New Unblocked Manager* (Gower, Aldershot, 1996).

Task one

Your group is asked to work with other groups to give ONE presentation entitled:

ECONOMIC PROSPECTS – A FIVE-YEAR VIEW

The presentation should cover current economic trends and how you see them developing over the next five years.

These are the rules:

1. Your group must work on its own for the first 25 minutes of the task. Thereafter you may work together as you wish.

2. The presentation must be complete in 30 minutes.

3. During the first 25 minutes of the exercise one member of your group may leave at any time for meetings and so on but the other members of the group must stay in the room that you have been allocated.

4. The presentation must last exactly 5 minutes.

Task two: Group A

Your group is asked to work with other groups to give ONE presentation entitled:

SOCIAL PROSPECTS – A FIVE-YEAR VIEW.

These are the rules:

1. Your group must work on its own for the first 15 minutes of the task. Thereafter you may work together as you wish.

2. The presentation must be complete in 20 minutes.

3. One member of your group may leave at any time for meetings and so on but the other members of the group must stay in the room that you have been allocated (for the first 15 minutes of the exercise).

4. The presentation must last exactly 5 minutes.

5. Your group is responsible for a segment lasting exactly 1 minute and 15 seconds on SOCIAL TRENDS IN YOUNG PEOPLE. You should mention only three important themes. You will present first.

Reproduced from *Developing Your People: Easy-to-use activities for improving management skills*
by Mike Woodcock and Dave Francis, Gower, Aldershot

Task two: Group B

Your group is asked to work with other groups to give ONE presentation entitled:

SOCIAL PROSPECTS – A FIVE-YEAR VIEW

These are the rules:

1. Your group must work on its own for the first 15 minutes of the task. Thereafter you may work together as you wish.

2. The presentation must be complete in 20 minutes.

3. One member of your group may leave at any time for meetings and so on but the other members of the group must stay in the room that you have been allocated (for the first 15 minutes of the exercise).

4. The presentation must last exactly 5 minutes.

5. Your group is responsible for a segment lasting exactly 1 minute and 15 seconds on SOCIAL TRENDS IN OLDER PEOPLE (60+). You should mention only three important themes. You will present second.

Task two: Group C

Your group is asked to work with other groups to give ONE presentation entitled:

SOCIAL PROSPECTS – A FIVE-YEAR VIEW

These are the rules:

1. Your group must work on its own for the first 15 minutes of the task. Thereafter you may work together as you wish.

2. The presentation must be complete in 20 minutes.

3. One member of your group may leave at any time for meetings and so on but the other members of the group must stay in the room that you have been allocated (for the first 15 minutes of the exercise).

4. The presentation must last exactly 5 minutes.

5. Your group is responsible for a segment lasting exactly 1 minute and 15 seconds on SOCIAL TRENDS IN CITIES. You should mention only three important themes. You will present third.

Task two: Group D

Your group is asked to work with other groups to give ONE presentation entitled:

SOCIAL PROSPECTS – A FIVE-YEAR VIEW

These are the rules:

1. Your group must work on its own for the first 15 minutes of the task. Thereafter you may work together as you wish.

2. The presentation must be complete in 20 minutes.

3. One member of your group may leave at any time for meetings and so on but the other members of the group must stay in the room that you have been allocated (for the first 15 minutes of the exercise).

4. The presentation must last exactly 5 minutes.

5. Your group is responsible for a segment lasting exactly 1 minute and 15 seconds on SOCIAL TRENDS IN RURAL COMMUNITIES. You should mention only three important themes. You will present fourth.

31

Coaching workbook

Objectives

- To explore the role of coaching within personal development planning.
- To present a step-by-step process for managing a coaching initiative.
- To increase awareness of job-integrated training methodologies.

Group size

Unlimited (but workbook is usually used on a one-to-one basis).

Time required

30 minutes to introduce.

Materials required

1. Task sheet 31.1: Coaching workbook.
2. OHPs 31.1 and 31.2.

Description

To structure the process of coaching others.

Method		Approx time
1	Introduce the topic of coaching using OHP 31.1 to structure the input.	10 mins
2	Hand out copies of Task sheet 31.1: Coaching workbook and talk through the 15-step process with the group.	10 mins
3	Encourage members of the group to raise questions.	5 mins
4	Invite participants to complete page 1 of Task sheet 31.1.	5 mins
	(Optional) After the coaching process has been completed (normally 2–4 weeks later), a review meeting can be held.	

Coaching workbook

Coaching is the process of building an individual's capability once he or she has acquired relevant basic skills.

On the following pages you will find a 15-step coaching process. Use this on a real-life case.

Fill in the four boxes below as indicated.

1. The coach will be ...

2. The person being coached will be ...

3. The objectives of the coaching process will be ...

4. The plan for coaching begins .... (date) and is intended to be complete on .... (date)

Coaching process

Directions

Work through the 15 steps as indicated.

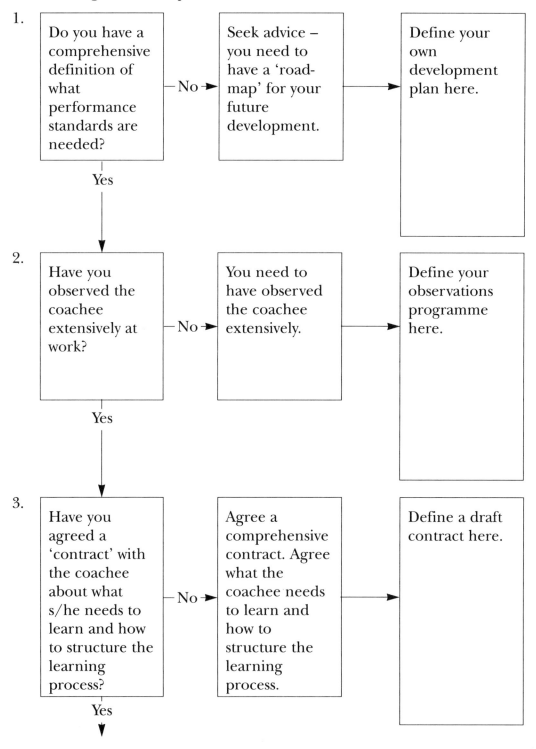

1.

| Do you have a comprehensive definition of what performance standards are needed? | –No→ | Seek advice – you need to have a 'road-map' for your future development. | → | Define your own development plan here. |

Yes ↓

2.

| Have you observed the coachee extensively at work? | –No→ | You need to have observed the coachee extensively. | → | Define your observations programme here. |

Yes ↓

3.

| Have you agreed a 'contract' with the coachee about what s/he needs to learn and how to structure the learning process? | –No→ | Agree a comprehensive contract. Agree what the coachee needs to learn and how to structure the learning process. | → | Define a draft contract here. |

Yes ↓

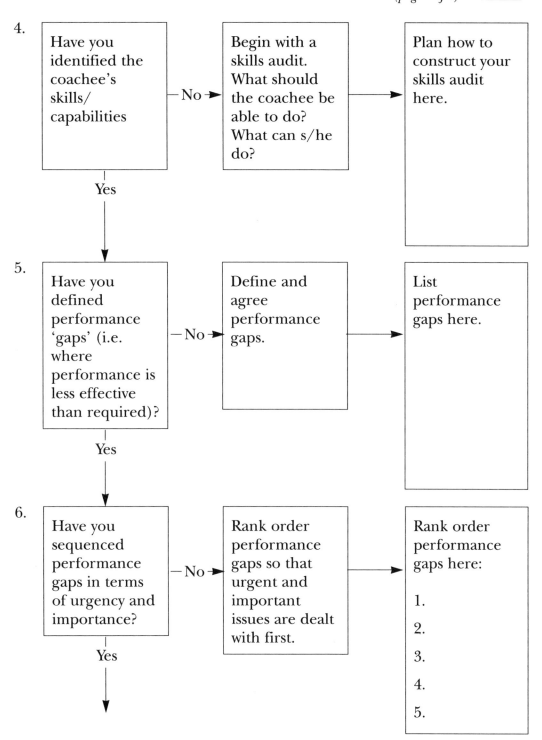

4. Have you identified the coachee's skills/capabilities

— No → Begin with a skills audit. What should the coachee be able to do? What can s/he do?

→ Plan how to construct your skills audit here.

Yes

5. Have you defined performance 'gaps' (i.e. where performance is less effective than required)?

— No → Define and agree performance gaps.

→ List performance gaps here.

Yes

6. Have you sequenced performance gaps in terms of urgency and importance?

— No → Rank order performance gaps so that urgent and important issues are dealt with first.

→ Rank order performance gaps here:

1.

2.

3.

4.

5.

Yes

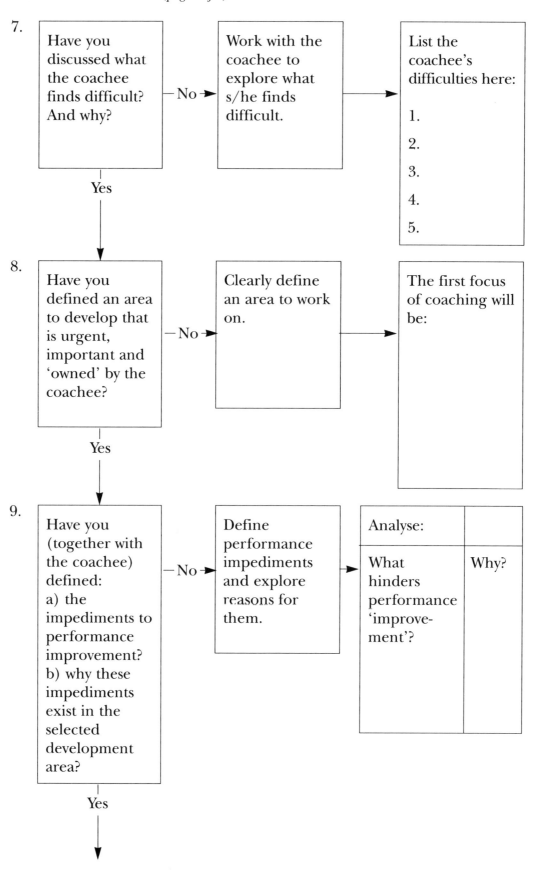

7.
| Have you discussed what the coachee finds difficult? And why? | —No→ | Work with the coachee to explore what s/he finds difficult. | → | List the coachee's difficulties here:

1.

2.

3.

4.

5. |

↓ Yes

8.
| Have you defined an area to develop that is urgent, important and 'owned' by the coachee? | —No→ | Clearly define an area to work on. | → | The first focus of coaching will be: |

↓ Yes

9.
| Have you (together with the coachee) defined:
a) the impediments to performance improvement?
b) why these impediments exist in the selected development area? | —No→ | Define performance impediments and explore reasons for them. | → | Analyse: | |
| | | | | What hinders performance 'improvement'? | Why? |

↓ Yes

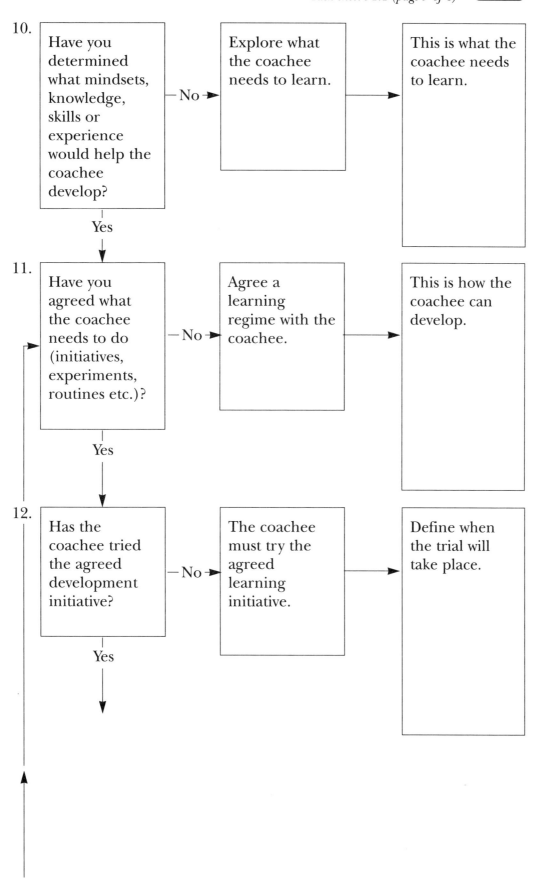

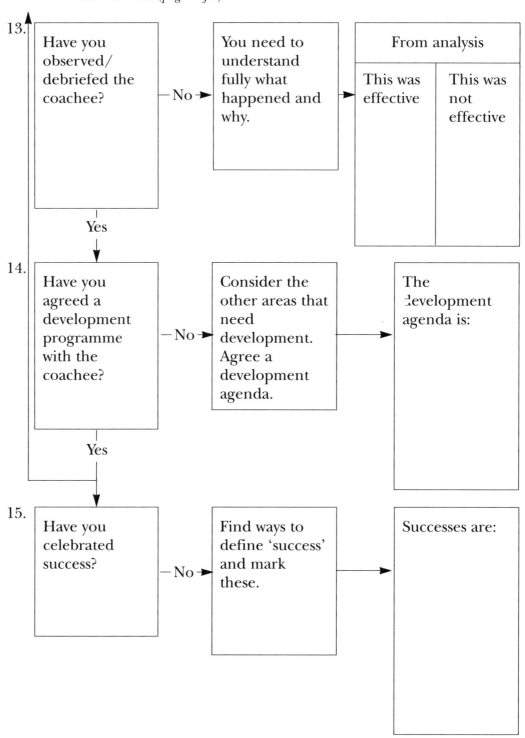

13. | Have you observed/debriefed the coachee? | — No → | You need to understand fully what happened and why. | → | From analysis |
    This was effective | This was not effective

    Yes ↓

14. | Have you agreed a development programme with the coachee? | — No → | Consider the other areas that need development. Agree a development agenda. | → | The development agenda is: |

    Yes ↓

15. | Have you celebrated success? | — No → | Find ways to define 'success' and mark these. | → | Successes are: |

1. COACHING ...

- Builds on instruction (assumes basic skills).

- Learning programme adapted to each individual.

- Personal blocks to competency must be identified.

- Current skills enhanced.

- Deals with every aspect of performance (knowledge, skills, style, personality etc.)

- Coach is the guardian of standards.

- Begins with a contract about what development is needed.

- Aim is to improve performance today.

2. 15 STEPS TO EFFECTIVE COACHING

1. Define performance standards.

2. Observe.

3. 'Contract' how to manage learning.

4. Identify current skills.

5. Define performance gaps.

6. Identify development priorities.

7. Explore general difficulties.

8. Select a focus area.

9. Explore specific difficulties.

10. Determine what needs to change.

11. Agree how development can be managed.

12. Carry out a trial.

13. Review the trial.

14. Agree next steps.

15. Celebrate success.

32

Tools for developing managers

Objectives

- To improve skills in selecting appropriate 'tools' to achieve management development objectives.

- To assist in the evaluation of different methods and techniques of management development.

- To broaden the view of management development methods and techniques.

Group size

Any number of groups with three to seven members.

Time required

1 hour 30 minutes.

Materials required

1. Task sheet 32.1: Management development problem and individual worksheet.

2. Task sheet 32.2: Group worksheet.

3. Handout 32.1: The experts' ranking.

4. Task sheet 32.3: Management development problem: analysis sheet.

5. Task sheet 32.4: Management development: personal planning.

Description

There are many 'tools' available to develop management potential. In this activity, the members of a group or team share their views about management development using a problem-solving task. Emphasize that the problem is merely a vehicle for discussion and that the activity is completed only when the insights are applied to the actual work group.

Method		Approx time
1	Give participants a copy of Task sheet 32.1: Management development problem and individual worksheet; ask them to complete it individually.	15 mins
2	Divide participants into groups and ask each group to attempt to reach consensus on the rankings and fill in the group's ranking on Task sheet 32.2: Group worksheet.	45 mins
3	After reviewing Handout 32.1: The experts' ranking, ask participants to fill out Task sheet 32.3: Management development problem: analysis sheet and review the activity. Using Task sheet 32.4, participants plan their personal development needs.	30 mins

Management development problem

Below you will find a short description of a management development problem. After reading it, rank the 15 possible action steps in order of importance. Do this individually and then discuss the same problem with the group for 40 minutes to arrive at a consensus ranking. Finally, compare your scores with those of the 'expert' panel and evaluate your results.

The problem

Rachel Smith is a 30-year-old manager who has recently been promoted to lead a business unit with 105 staff within a medium-sized electronics corporation. She will have much broader responsibilities than in her previous job. She has a degree in history and has proved to be an outstandingly effective production manager. However, she lacks any formal management education and feels that her previous experience has been narrow.

Reproduced from *Developing Your People: Easy-to-use activities for improving management skills* by Mike Woodcock and Dave Francis, Gower, Aldershot

Individual worksheet

Although you do not have sufficient information to make a detailed assessment, rank the 15 items below in order of what you believe would be the most useful development experiences for Rachel Smith. If Rachel could have only one of the experiences, which would you advise? Rank this number 1. If she could have another, rank it number 2, and so on.

Individual ranking

1. Course in business finance at a well-regarded business school (2 weeks). _____

2. Coaching session with boss each week (2 hours per week). _____

3. Study tour of other electronics companies (1 week). _____

4. Course in interpersonal skills and team building (1 week). _____

5. Time to read management textbooks (60 hours). _____

6. Observation of her senior team at work (12 hours). _____

7. Workshop with all members of her senior team to develop a business strategy, led by an experienced facilitator (3 days). _____

8. Attendance at conference on 'Electronics Futures: A 10-Year Vision' ($2^1/_2$ days). _____

9. Personal consultant help on use of time (1 half-day weekly for 8 weeks). _____

10. Course entitled 'Yoga for Stress Management' (4 days). _____

11. Seminar on 'The Sociology of Emerging Organizations' (4 days). _____

12. Project: write paper on 'The General Management Role' which will be discussed with a leading academic (1 week to write paper and 3 hours' seminar). _____

13. Temporary assignment as Marketing Director's Assistant (3 weeks). _____

14. Attend intensive outdoor course on 'Practical Leadership' (5 days). _____

15. Regular meetings with other, new general managers to discuss common problems, led by experienced facilitator (2 half-days per month). _____

Group worksheet

As a group, you are to reach consensus on a ranking for each of the 15 items listed on the individual work sheet. If Rachel Smith could have only one of the experiences, which would you advise? This is to be ranked number 1. If she could have another, this is to be ranked number 2, and so on.

Consensus decisions are often difficult to achieve. The following guidelines may help you:

1. Set an outline timetable and process.

2. See whether you can find a way to identify key issues or principles before you become involved in details.

3. Plan democratic procedures for sharing ideas before you debate controversial issues.

4. Try to listen carefully to one another and seek common ground.

5. Be less prepared to compromise on matters of principle, but be more flexible on details.

6. Check frequently for agreement and redesign the group process if you become stuck.

Although you do not have sufficient information to make a detailed assessment, rank the 15 items below in order of what you believe would be the most useful development experiences for Rachel Smith.

		Group ranking
1.	Course in business finance at a well-regarded business school (2 weeks).	_____
2.	Coaching session with boss each week (2 hours per week).	_____
3.	Study tour of other electronics companies (1 week).	_____
4.	Course in interpersonal skills and team building (1 week).	_____
5.	Time to read management textbooks (60 hours).	_____
6.	Observation of her senior team at work (12 hours).	_____
7.	Workshop with all members of her senior team to develop a business strategy led by an experienced facilitator (3 days).	_____
8.	Attendance at conference on 'Electronics Futures: A 10-Year Vision' ($2^{1}/_{2}$ days).	_____

9. Personal consultant help on use of time (1 half-day weekly for 8 weeks). _____

10. Course entitled 'Yoga for Stress Management' (4 days). _____

11. Seminar on 'The Sociology of Emerging Organizations' (4 days). _____

12. Project: write paper on 'The General Management Role' which will be discussed with a leading academic (1 week to write paper and 3 hours' seminar). _____

13. Temporary assignment as Marketing Director's Assistant (3 weeks). _____

14. Attend intensive outdoor course on 'Practical Leadership' (5 days). _____

15. Regular meetings with other, new general managers to discuss common problems, led by experienced facilitator (2 half-days per month). _____

Reproduced from *Developing Your People: Easy-to-use activities for improving management skills*
by Mike Woodcock and Dave Francis, Gower, Aldershot

The experts' ranking

The management development problem was considered by 47 management development specialists. Their rationale and ranking are listed below. You can compare your ranking with theirs by computing the difference on each item and adding these sums together. Of course, there are no 'right' answers, and much depends on the individual involved. However, these rankings can be used to stimulate discussion.

Rationale

The experts felt that initially Rachel Smith needed support as well as intensive development of the concept of her new job – learning how to deal with day-by-day problems. Second, the manager would benefit from expanding her understanding of strategic vision and specific managerial skills which would be clearly relevant to her new job. Third, development of her interpersonal skills and learning through participation in management projects would add depth and bring new insight. Lastly, she should be introduced to general management topics. A brief rationale follows for each item.

Experts' rankings

1. 2-hour coaching session with boss each week.
   - Essential for support and immediate development.

2. Regular meetings with other new general managers to discuss common problems, led by experienced facilitator (2 half-days per month).
   - Very important support and learning vehicle.

3. Participation in workshop with all members of senior team, led by an experienced facilitator to develop business strategy (3 days).
   - To clarify direction and develop communication.

4. Consultant help on use of time (1 half-day weekly for 4 weeks).
   - For relevant coaching, very practical.

5. Write paper on 'The General Management Role' which will be discussed with a leading academic (1 week and 3 hours).
   - Provides intellectual foundation for new job.

6. Study tour of other electronics companies (1 week).
   - An invaluable basis for benchmarking.

7. Conference on 'Electronics Futures' (2¹/₂ days).
   - Would encourage much relevant discussion and develop contacts.

8. Course in interpersonal skills and team building (1 week).
   - For personal development and review.

9. Time to read management textbooks (60 hours).
   - If well used, this could fit many ideas into context.

10. Outdoor course on 'Practical Leadership' (5 days).
    - To strengthen confidence and leadership skills.

11. Observation of senior team at work (12 hours).
    - Sets the context for her new job – will clarify boss's expectations.

12. Course in business finance (2 weeks).
    - For management development in a vital area of need.

13. Temporary assignment as Marketing Director's Assistant (3 weeks).
    - Will strengthen expertise in a weak area.

14. Seminar on 'The Sociology of Emerging Organizations' (4 days).
    - May have high degree of relevance.

15. Course entitled 'Yoga for Stress Management' (4 days).
    - Could be valuable but perhaps should be followed in own time.

Reproduced from *Developing Your People: Easy-to-use activities for improving management skills* by Mike Woodcock and Dave Francis, Gower, Aldershot

Management development problem: analysis sheet

NOTE: When calculating differences, ignore pluses and minuses.

	Step 1: Your Individual Ranking	Step 2: The Group's Ranking	Step 3: Difference Between Step 1 & Step 2	Step 4: Experts' Ranking	Step 5: Difference Between Step 1 & Step 4	Step 6: Difference Between Step 2 and Step 4
Coaching with boss				1		
Meetings with other managers				2		
Participation in strategy workshop				3		
Consultant help				4		
Paper on 'General Management Role'				5		
Study tour of electronics companies				6		
Conference 'Electronic Futures'				7		
Interpersonal skills and team-building course				8		
Reading textbooks				9		
Outdoor course on 'Practical Leadership'				10		
Observation of senior team				11		
Business finance course				12		
Marketing assignment				13		
Sociology seminar				14		
Yoga course				15		
Totals (the lower the score the better)						

Step 5 total = Your Score _____

Step 6 total = Group Score _____

	Group Number					
Complete the following steps and insert the scores under your group's number.	1	2	3	4	5	6
Step 6: **Team Score**						
Step 7: **Average Individual Score** Add up all the individual scores (Step 5) in the group and divide by the number of people in the group.						
Step 8: **Gain Score** The difference between the group score and the average individual score. If the group score is lower than the average individual score, the gain is plus. If the group score is higher than the average individual score, the gain is minus.						
Step 9: **Lowest Individual Score** in the group.						
Step 10: **Number of Individual Scores** that are lower than the group score.						

Management development personal planning

Personal development needs

Consider your own development needs and then rank the 15 action steps in terms of their relevance to you and your job. Again, rank the 15 items in order of importance. You will notice that these are not identical with the action steps in the case study.

		Your personal ranking
1.	Course in business finance.	_____
2.	Counselling from boss.	_____
3.	Study tour of other companies.	_____
4.	Course in interpersonal skills.	_____
5.	Time to read management textbooks.	_____
6.	Observation of senior team at work.	_____
7.	Introduction to skills of performance management.	_____
8.	Participation in team-building session.	_____
9.	Consultant help on use of time.	_____
10.	Course on 'Yoga for Stress Management'.	_____
11.	Seminar on the sociology of organizations.	_____
12.	Project on topic of your choice.	_____
13.	Temporary assignment to department of your choice.	_____
14.	Training in leadership theory.	_____
15.	Regular meetings with other managers on your level.	_____

Reproduced from *Developing Your People: Easy-to-use activities for improving management skills* by Mike Woodcock and Dave Francis, Gower, Aldershot

Task sheet 32.4 (page 2 of 2)

After you have completed your personal assessment, share the results with others in your group.

A personal action plan completes the session. The format below may be helpful.

Personal Development Needs	Ways to Achieve

33

Development review process

Objectives

- To provide a structured process for reviewing performance.
- To use performance review to clarify development needs.
- To develop skills in planning an individual development programme.

Group size

Unlimited (but the process is usually used on a one-to-one basis).

Time required

30 minutes' briefing, then as required.

Materials required

1. Task sheet 33.1: Development review process workbook.
2. OHP 33.1.

Description

This activity provides a format for a manager to review the performance of a subordinate and produce a development plan. It can be used by a manager working alone or as the framework for an organizational development review process.

If the Development review process (DRP) is used as the basis of an organization-wide process each step should be evaluated before use to ensure conformity with other systems for appraisal, evaluation, succession planning and so on.

Method		Approx time
1	Managers are briefed on the step-by-step process. Use OHP 33.1 to introduce the approach. Each manager should receive a copy of Task sheet 33.1: Development review process workbook at this stage.	30 mins
2	Managers use the DRP process as described.	as required

Development review process workbook

Use this workbook to structure a development review. Work through the process step by step.

Name of Reviewee ....

Date of Review ....

Are you familiar with the company's development review system?	◄–No–►	Contact manager of human resources	Action Required

    │
   Yes
    │
    ▼

Do you feel you have the necessary skills?	◄–No–►	Discuss with your manager – agree a training plan.	Action Required

    │
   Yes
    │
    ▼

Have you prepared a timetable to gather data and conduct the review?	◄–No–►	Read entire process. Establish a timetable.	Action Required

    │
   Yes
    │
    ▼

T

Have you collected performance data from colleagues, customers and other managers?	◄–No–►	Develop a questionnaire for colleagues, customers (internal and/or external) and managers. Collect data and conduct follow-up interview.	Action Required

↓ Yes

Have you analysed the data systematically?	◄–No–►	Review all data to identify:	Action Required

a) Existing strengths.

b) Areas where performance can be enhanced.

c) Areas for improvement.

d) New skills/ behaviours needed.

↓ Yes

Has the reviewee prepared?	◄–No–►	Brief reviewee. Provide a structure for her/him to prepare.	Action Required

↓ Yes

Do you have ideas about how performance gaps could be overcome?	◄–No–►	Discuss with Human Resources manager and/or training specialist.	Action Required

↓ Yes

Reproduced from *Developing Your People: Easy-to-use activities for improving management skills* by Mike Woodcock and Dave Francis, Gower, Aldershot

Have you planned the development review meeting?	◄–No–►Arrange a venue and set aside at least 90 minutes.	Action Required

Yes

Have you developed an agenda for the meeting?	◄–No–►Plan an agenda. Include:	Action Required

a) Performance review.

b) Identification of areas for enhancement and development.

c) Reviewee's interests.

d) Development process planning.

e) Action plan.

Yes

You are ready!

Development review meeting start

Have interruptions been prevented? ◄–No–►Take measures to prevent interruptions.

Yes

Is the reviewee at ease? ◄–No–►Talk about his/her feelings. Clarify expectations. Emphasize the *development* purpose of the meeting.

Yes

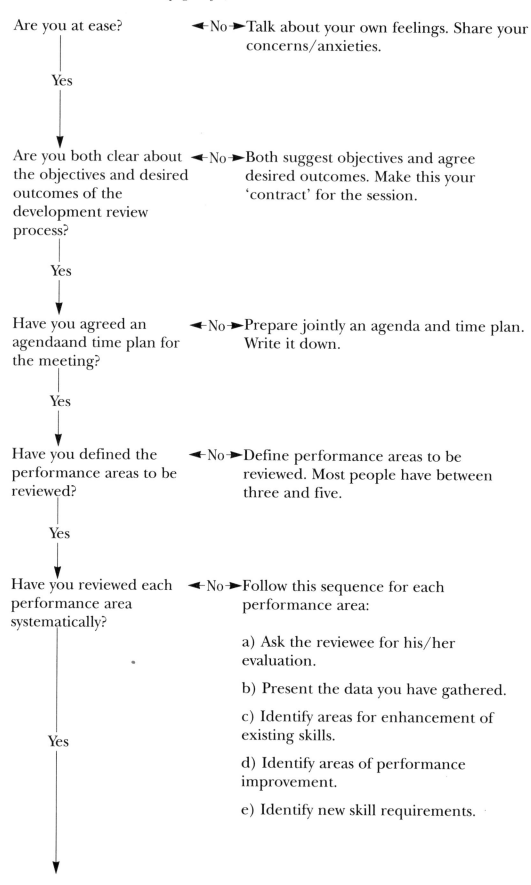

Are you at ease? ◄─No─► Talk about your own feelings. Share your concerns/anxieties.

Yes

Are you both clear about the objectives and desired outcomes of the development review process? ◄─No─► Both suggest objectives and agree desired outcomes. Make this your 'contract' for the session.

Yes

Have you agreed an agenda and time plan for the meeting? ◄─No─► Prepare jointly an agenda and time plan. Write it down.

Yes

Have you defined the performance areas to be reviewed? ◄─No─► Define performance areas to be reviewed. Most people have between three and five.

Yes

Have you reviewed each performance area systematically? ◄─No─► Follow this sequence for each performance area:

a) Ask the reviewee for his/her evaluation.

b) Present the data you have gathered.

c) Identify areas for enhancement of existing skills.

d) Identify areas of performance improvement.

e) Identify new skill requirements.

Yes

400

T

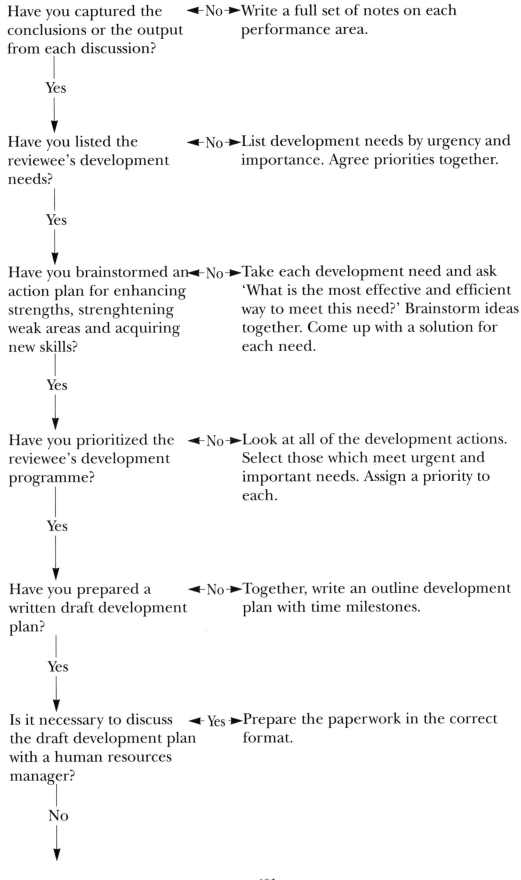

Have you captured the conclusions or the output from each discussion? ◄–No–►Write a full set of notes on each performance area.

Yes

Have you listed the reviewee's development needs? ◄–No–►List development needs by urgency and importance. Agree priorities together.

Yes

Have you brainstormed an ◄–No–►Take each development need and ask action plan for enhancing strengths, strenghtening weak areas and acquiring new skills? 'What is the most effective and efficient way to meet this need?' Brainstorm ideas together. Come up with a solution for each need.

Yes

Have you prioritized the reviewee's development programme? ◄–No–►Look at all of the development actions. Select those which meet urgent and important needs. Assign a priority to each.

Yes

Have you prepared a written draft development plan? ◄–No–►Together, write an outline development plan with time milestones.

Yes

Is it necessary to discuss the draft development plan with a human resources manager? ◄–Yes–►Prepare the paperwork in the correct format.

No

401

Have you summarized the ◄-No-► Go through the agenda and check that
meeting with the reviewee? you have covered all items. Summarize
key points.

Yes

Have you agreed a follow- ◄-No-► Set time aside in both your diaries for
up process to take follow-up sessions.
initiatives and monitor
progress?

Yes

Have you received ◄-No-► Ask for feedback on areas that you could
feedback on your style improve next time.
of conducting a
development review?

Yes

Agree what both of you will do next.

The Reviewer's Action Plan	
Actions	Date
The Reviewee's Action Plan	
Actions	Date

DEVELOPMENT REVIEW PROCESS

How to make it successful...

1. Follow the steps – each builds on the one before.

2. Collect comprehensive performance data before the meeting.

3. Adopt a collaborative 'win–win' approach.

4. Agree a 'contract' about desired outcomes and ground rules early on.

5. Have equal air-time when discussing issues.

6. Deal with performance problems positively and respectfully.

7. Conclude with a manageable action plan targeted on priorities.

403

34

Customer orientation index

Objectives

- To provide a structured methodology for assessing the degree of customer orientation of a department or organization.

- To assist managers to determine their personal commitment to building a customer-driven organization.

- To heighten understanding of techniques for increasing customer orientation.

Group size

1. This activity can be used by any manager as the definition of 'customer' includes internal as well as external users of products and/or services supplied by the manager's department or organization.

2. In the form shown in this activity the information collected is used for survey feedback. For example, all of the employees in a department could complete the survey and then discuss the data generated at a departmental meeting. However, the Customer orientation index can be readily adapted for use on training programmes, team-building events and individual coaching programmes.

3. There is no limit to the number of people who can participate at any one time.

Time required

1 hour 30 minutes.

Materials required

1. Task sheet 34.1: Customer orientation index.
2. Task sheet 34.2: Customer orientation index worksheet.
3. OHPs 34.1 and OHP 34.2.
4. Flipchart.

Description

The Customer orientation index (COI) is used as a device for consciousness raising and preliminary diagnosis. The COI is not intended as a full survey as the questions asked are broad and would need to be customized to meet the specific requirements of the organization being surveyed. However, the diagnostic framework suggested provides the basis for a wide-ranging enquiry.

Method		Approx time
1	Introduce the activity by referring to the objectives (above) and introducing the topic of customer service. OHP 34.1: Customer Service can be used as a structure for this introductory session.	10 mins
2	Lead the group in agreeing a definition of the organization being assessed and the client group – as defined in the text.	5 mins
3	Each individual privately completes Task sheet 34.1: Customer orientation index.	10 mins
4	Summarize the four areas of the COI by referring to OHP 34.2. Emphasize that all four areas must be strong for customer orientation to be high.	5 mins

Method		Approx time
5	Distribute Task sheet 34.2: Customer orientation index worksheet. Divide the group into sub-groups for the activity. A group of four is the ideal size. Completed questionnaires are scored and discussed as directed. The groups take turns helping each member improve his/her customer-service orientation. Brainstorming ideas on a flipchart is often useful.	45 mins for a group of 4
6	Gather all participating groups together and collect views. List key ideas on a flipchart. These ideas may be typed and provided as a handout from the session.	10 mins
7	Conclude the activity with sub-groups coming together to discuss action points.	10 mins

Customer orientation index

This short questionnaire will help you determine to what extent your organization/department is oriented towards understanding and meeting the needs of your customers. Before you begin, agree with your colleagues a clear definition of 'your organization' (box 1) and the 'customer group' you are assessing (box 2).

1.

For the purpose of this questionnaire 'our organization' is …

2.

We are considering our relationship with this customer group …

Instructions

Consider the behaviours below and decide whether you are performing the activity (column 1) and how well you are performing the activity (column 2).

	1	2
BEHAVIOUR	Performed? Yes/No	How well? (mark out of 10)
1. We have asked representatives of the customer group what they want from us.		
2. We run 'focus groups' to find out what customers want from us.		
3. We actively seek comments, criticisms and complaints.		
4. All employees spend time talking to customers.		
5. We actively seek feedback on our successes in achieving a high level of customer service.		
6. We formally evaluate customer comments, criticisms and complaints.		
7. We list our successes and work out how we can get it right more often.		
8. We have developed a 'theory' of what we need to do to provide a high level of customer service.		
9. We have a regular mechanism which forces us to review whether we are achieving customer satisfaction.		
10. Our customer service performance goals are clearly spelt out.		

	1	2
BEHAVIOUR	Performed? Yes/No	How well? (mark out of 10)
11. Every member of the department has objectives which define customer service standards to be achieved.		
12. There are regular meetings at which our performance against customer service standards is reviewed.		
13. Staff are individually reviewed and appraised against customer service objectives.		
14. Groups meet to review customer complaints and find ways to overcome problems.		
15. Good practice learned from success is shared and widely practised.		
16. Staff are prepared 'to go the extra mile' to satisfy customers.		
17. We maintain open and friendly communication with customers.		
18. We keep our promises.		
19. When things go wrong we maintain positive supportive relationships.		
20. We welcome the chance to put right our errors.		

Customer orientation index worksheet

Discuss the COI results. If appropriate, consider each individual's scores separately. Brainstorm on a flipchart how you can improve the customer service orientation of the department/unit. Record ideas below.

1. The strongest areas of customer orientation are:

2. The weakest areas of customer orientation are:

3. These practical activities could be undertaken to improve customer service orientation:

4. Consider each of the activities listed under number 3 and try to find good reasons why each activity should not be undertaken.

Suggested activity	Reasons why unworkable or inappropriate

5. Consider the remaining workable suggestions:

What needs to be done?	By whom	How	By when

1. CUSTOMER SERVICE

- A customer is anyone who uses the products/services that you produce.

- Customers are internal (within your own organization) and external (end-users).

- Some groups have multiple customers – each needs to be considered separately.

- Historically departments have not seen themselves as a link in a chain of suppliers and customers.

- Understanding and meeting suppliers' needs is an essential building block of organizational effectiveness.

2. FOUR AREAS OF CUSTOMER ORIENTATION

1. Understanding customer wants and needs (Questions 1–5)

2. Defining customer service (Questions 6–10)

3. Delivering customer service (Questions 11–15)

4. Adopting a customer service orientation (Questions 16–20)

35

Customer decision process analysis

Objectives

- To explain a systematic approach for analysing a customer's decision-making process.

- To develop skills in analysing customers' needs.

- To heighten awareness of the need to focus on customers' psychological processes.

- To provide a framework for an effective marketing intervention.

Group size

1. There is no limit to the number of participants who can work on this activity at any one time.

2. The activity is most useful when used by an intact team and it can form the basis for an extensive project which maps customer decision processes for different market segments, and even looks at the decision-making processes of those who decide not to buy, or buy elsewhere.

3. The methodology is a valuable tool for managers and can be taught on training programmes, action learning sessions and so on. In this case participants' examples of 'real-life' situations should be used for the practical work.

Time required

1 hour 10 minutes (minimum).

Materials required

- Task sheet 35.1: Customer decision process analysis: explanation and worksheet.
- OHP 35.1.

Description

This activity can be used to analyse the decision-making processes of 'end-user' customers and 'internal' customers. For example, a firm may be selling a carpet-cleaning service and will use customer decision process analysis (CDPA) to explore how people with dirty carpets decide which cleaning firm to employ. Also, within the firm the accounts function (for example) will use the CDPA to review what line managers want and need in terms of accounting information.

	Method	Approx time
1	Introduce the concept of CDPA using OHP 35.1.	10 mins
2	Form groups of three to five participants and give out Task sheet 35.1: The Customer decision process analysis: explanation and worksheet. Ask them to complete the example task as directed and share the results (the facilitator acts as coach).	30 mins
3	Groups then use the CDPA method 'for real' – either on one person's issue or a team issue.	minimum 30 mins

Customer decision process analysis: explanation and worksheet

Ask any manager what are the key attributes of organizational success and the chances are that they will include 'superior customer service' as one of the top characteristics. But what do we mean by 'superior customer service'? Obviously, a firm can train staff to be polite, responsive and quick to put errors right. However, this can be done by all firms, and organizations that seek to excel in customer service must go one step further and strive to understand the customer more fully and deeply than their competitors.

Customer decision process analysis (CDPA) is a method for understanding how customers make decisions and, most importantly, for identifying their key decision points. Deeper understanding of the decision points enables a marketing strategy to be determined which focuses on influencing the potential customer just at the point when they are making up their mind.

So what does a CDPA look like? Let us take a very simple example. It is a hot day and a tourist begins to wonder whether they would like to have an ice cream. The decision process (which is an inner dialogue in the person's head) may look like that shown in Figure 35.1.

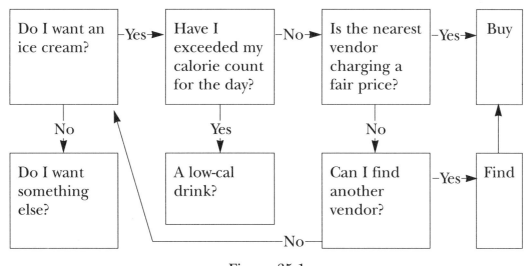

Figure 35.1

As you can see, all we have done is to flow-chart the decision-making process, but simply doing this makes certain things clear. These include:

● Vendors must signal comparative value for money.

● It would make sense to have a low-calorie option for weight watchers.

- Vendors should (if they can) make the concept of an ice cream more attractive.

Internal customers

You can often adapt the CDPA for internal customers. Let us assume that you are the Head of Human Resource Management in a medium-sized organization and wish to introduce an improved performance review system. You can see this as a 'product' and the managers you are seeking to influence as the 'market'. Figure 35.2 shows a simplified example of a CDPA for introducing an improved performance review system.

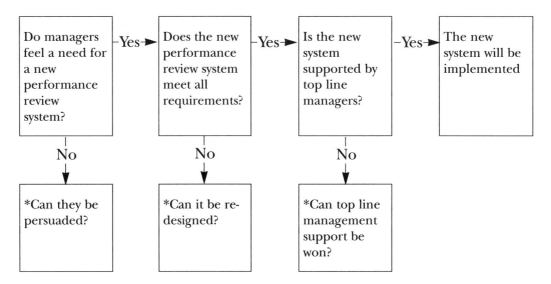

Figure 35.2

Even from this simplified CDPA you can see that key questions emerge (marked with *) and it is easy to imagine how the sponsor of the new performance review process would be better able to predict difficulties and resolve them early.

Your tasks

1. It is now time for you to practise using the CDPA technique yourself. This is best done in a small group. Take a sheet of flipchart paper and develop an imaginary CDPA for a person who is considering whether to buy (for the first time) a kitchen blender. If possible share the example charts with other teams working on the same project to fine-tune your technique.

2. Now take a real customer (perhaps a representative of a customer group or market segment) and develop a CDPA of how they would choose to buy your product and you as a supplier. Use the following procedure:

   a) Be as objective as possible. Interview customers or hold focus groups if you can.

   b) Try to identify all the possible influences on customers' buying decisions.

   c) List the influences in terms of closeness to the final purchase decision. General influences (for example television lifestyle advertising) are placed at the top of the chart and immediate influences (for example attitude of the sales clerk) are placed at the bottom of the chart.

   d) Show the interactions between factors with arrows and so on. Prepare your diagram like a flow chart or decision tree.

   e) Some influences will be more important than others – these can be shown graphically (for example with the use of colour).

   f) Whenever possible check your draft chart with actual customers to assess whether your analysis is perceived to be accurate.

   g) Consider the implications of your analysis for the department or organization.

Reproduced from *Developing Your People: Easy-to-use activities for improving management skills* by Mike Woodcock and Dave Francis, Gower, Aldershot

CUSTOMER DECISION PROCESS ANALYSIS

* Customers make multiple decisions about whether to buy, from whom to buy and when to buy.

* Firms need to understand the customer's decision-making process *in depth.*

* A flow chart is a simple, effective way to increase understanding.

* Whenever possible the process needs to be validated with actual customers.

* Implications and ideas need to be identified separately.

36

Internal customer survey workbook

Objectives

- To develop skills in surveying the needs and wants of internal 'customers'.

- To provide data for improving management performance.

- To undertake a comprehensive audit of current effectiveness.

- To advise departmental/unit action plans.

Group size

The Internal customer survey may be undertaken either alone or with a management team. Before undertaking the process managers are advised to gain the active support of their own manager.

Time required

Approximately 1 day (elapsed time).

Materials required

Task sheet 36.1: Customer survey workbook.

Description

This activity provides a straightforward technique for gathering data on how customers perceive the effectiveness of a specific department.

The Internal customer survey uses the techniques of survey feedback as a methodology. Survey feedback is one of the most useful interventions that can be made and, in this case, the manager collects and processes the data on his or her own area of responsibility. In essence the idea is straightforward: valid data are collected on relevant issues and fed back to those responsible for taking initiatives. This means that research and feedback should be dispassionate, objective, value-free and thorough.

In this activity customer survey feedback is given in three ways:

1. Feedback to individuals.

2. Feedback to teams.

3. Feedback to interdependent teams.

Method		Approx time
1	This activity is designed to be undertaken by a manager working alone or with his/her management team. Introduce the Customer survey workbook to the individual or team about to undertake the survey and explain the rationale and the structure of the workbook. This is described in Task sheet 36.1.	10 mins
2	Give each participant a copy of the survey and invite them to discuss how they can apply the process to their own team. Facilitate an action planning session and encourage the group to set a timetable for completion of the tasks described in the text.	30 mins

---

1. For a further explanation see *Survey Guided Development* (three volumes) by J. Franklin, A. Wissler and G. Spencer (University Associates, San Diego, CA, 1977).

Customer survey workbook

Just as firms find it necessary to collect data from their customers, so departments and teams within organizations need to find out exactly how their internal customers perceive their strengths and weaknesses.

The Customer survey enables you to:

- Undertake a comprehensive audit of current effectiveness.

- Identify strengths.

- Identify weaknesses.

- Develop personal action plans.

- Devise departmental/unit action plans.

The Customer survey may be undertaken either alone or with your management team. Prior to undertaking the process, managers are advised to gain the active support of their own manager.

Each step builds on previous work. You are advised to tackle the Customer survey in the sequence suggested. It involves five steps:

1. List all your internal customers. Select those that you wish to survey.

2. Find out what key customers want, using the Customer survey.

3. Define the gap between what is currently offered and what is desired. Identify those things that, if done badly, will create a 'feel bad' reaction and those things that, if done well, will delight the customer.

4. Map existing processes across departments. Simplify processes to remove unnecessary or wasteful elements and decide who manages processes and sub-processes.

5. Agree a 'service contract' which specifies deliverables. Establish what behaviours from your staff are needed. Set up a measuring and monitoring system.

The Customer survey workbook will take you through these five steps. The aim is to provide the data needed for a comprehensive review of managerial and departmental effectiveness.

Step one: identify your customers

Purpose: To identify your customers and select those that you wish to survey.

List all your internal customers and complete the analysis.

Internal Customers	How *important* is the interface in terms of your department's effectiveness? (1 = low, 5 = high)	How *satisfactory* is the interface? (1 = low, 5 = high)	Select important internal customers with whom the relationship could be improved

Step two: survey key customers

Purpose: To collect valid data about your performance from key customers.

You should use the 'sensing interview' approach to collect data. Sensing interviews take between 45 minutes and 90 minutes and should follow this pattern:

- Photocopy the interview schedule for each respondent.

- Put the respondent at ease by being relaxed yourself.

- Explain the purpose of the interview (emphasize that it is not an assessment of the respondent).

- Ask for questions or comment.

- Ask the interview questions and record the comments.

- Conclude with thanks. Say what will happen to the data.

Task sheet 36.1 (page 4 of 8)

Customer survey sensing interview questions

Sensing Interview Record Sheet Number ....

1. What aspects of our department's performance do you consider entirely satisfactory?

2. From your observation, what would you say are the strengths of our department?

3. What would our department have to do differently to make us excellent?

4. What practical actions should we take to improve our performance to you as a customer?

    a)

    b)

426

c)

d)

e)

5.   What feedback do you have for me in my role?

Things that I do which help our departments have a good relationship.

Things that I do which hinder our departments from having a good relationship.

Step three: identify performance gaps

Purpose: To define the gap between what is currently offered and what is desired.

Summary of data from key customer survey	These things are currently done less well than desired
These things currently delight the customer	The customer would like these new things to be done

Step four: process mapping

Purpose: Map existing processes across departments. Simplify processes to remove unnecessary or wasteful elements and decide who manages processes and sub-processes.

List across department processes	How could these be simplified or improved?	How should this be done?

Step five: improving interdepartmental relationships

Purpose: Agree a 'service contract' which specifies deliverables. Establish what behaviours from your staff are needed. Set up a measuring and monitoring system.

What services would you seek to provide? (Be specific, include measurable standards – 'deliverables')	What changes in behaviour are needed from your staff?	How can you establish a measuring and monitoring system?